Libby Purves is a novelist, journalist and broadcaster, who has presented the talk programme *Midweek* on BBC Radio 4 since 1983, as well as numerous other programmes. She was formerly the first regular woman (and youngest ever) presenter of *Today*. She is a main columnist on *The Times* and in 1999 was named the Granada 'What the Papers Say' columnist of the year and awarded an O.B.E. for services to journalism.

She lives in Suffolk with her husband — the broadcaster and writer Paul Heiney and their teenage son and daughter.

RADIO: A TRUE LOVE STORY

Libby Purves has loved the medium of radio all her life. She has worked with it for almost thirty years, and been made happy, angry, frustrated, delighted, amused, tender and furious from both sides of the microphone. In this revealing, at times hilarious memoir, Libby weaves together her own experiences with the story of radio's birth and development from the days of the romantic pioneers of 2LO, through the pirate era to the mushrooming of local radio and the development of aggressive news. In the process, she gives a very personal view of'the journey of British radio from John Reith to John Birt and beyond.

Books by Libby Purves
Published by The House of Ulverscroft:

LIBBY PURVES

RADIO:
A TRUE LOVE STORY

Complete and Unabridged

CHARNWOOD
Leicester

First published in Great Britain in 2002 by
Hodder & Stoughton
London

First Charnwood Edition
published 2003
by arrangement with
Hodder & Stoughton Limited
a division of Hodder Headline
London

British Library CIP Data

Purves, Libby, *1950 –*
    Radio: a true love story.—Large print ed.—
Charnwood library series
    1. Purves, Libby, *1950 –*
    2. Radio broadcasting—Great Britain—History
—20th century
    3. Large type books
    I. Title
    384.5′4′0941

ISBN 1–8439–5021–9

Published by
F. A. Thorpe (Publishing)
Anstey, Leicestershire

Set by Words & Graphics Ltd.
Anstey, Leicestershire
Printed and bound in Great Britain by
T. J. International Ltd., Padstow, Cornwall

This book is printed on acid-free paper

To the memory of Andy Wright, 1945–1997

'One might still have pattered about the benefits to invalids and aged folk; to those whose lot was cast in the loneliness of insularity in space or isolation of spirit.

About the amenities of town being carried to the country; about the myriad of voices of nature (nightingale included) being borne to the city street.

About the voice of leaders of thought and action coming to the fireside; the news of the world at the ear of the rustic.

About the Prime Minister speaking direct to the nation from his room in Downing Street; the King heard by his farthest and most solitary subject; the facts of great issues, hitherto distorted by partisan interpretation, now put directly and clearly before them; a return to the city-state of old.

All that and more' — *J. C. W. Reith, first Director-General of the BBC*

Contents

Introduction

The subtitle is not really a joke. There is something very personal about the medium of radio and I have loved it all my life, living with it in varying degrees of partnership for thirty years. Radio has made me happy, angry, frustrated, busy, awed, and — at certain memorable moments near the end of a long editing session — dizzily euphoric.

As a listener I have depended on it when I was weary at home with small children, dreading gales in the Atlantic, all but blind in a hospital bed, angry and hot in traffic-jams. Radio has introduced me to people, concepts, arguments, music and atmospheres that I would never have encountered otherwise. That awkward puritan John Reith was right when he said that the wireless is made to alleviate loneliness; and since loneliness is part of the human condition even in the midst of a busy life, that alone is worth loving it for. Radio reaches into your mind in a clear, pure, powerful stream of thought and emotion: it is closer to reading than to television or film, yet shares their ability to carry physical reality.

In Britain we have been lucky. An accident of history meant that radio grew up as a public service rather than a commercial venture, and this enabled it to flourish and experiment, fed by ideals that went beyond commercial profit or

1

state propaganda. Music and chat stations proliferate all over the globe and many of them are pleasant listening; but Britain's radio networks are replicated nowhere else in the world and could never be reinvented from scratch on a self-funding basis.

Certainly not now, in the age of television and Internet. BBC Radio has its faults — it can be cosy and smug and hidebound and singsong and gratuitously boring, and in recent years parts of it have abandoned some of the more demanding standards of taste and intelligence that it once set itself. But basically it is a marvel: direct communication, mind to intelligent mind, democratic, portable, open, and free.

Radio is the place where the best comedy is born because with its cheapness and speed it can be daring. From the Goons to Alan Partridge, Hancock to the *News Quiz*, it has led the way in inventive comic fantasy. In news, it produces more rigorous, questioning analysis than television does; again, its cheapness helps, and the emphasis on words and meanings rather than pictures. Its documentaries are more prolific, more varied, and often more memorable. Not only does the spoken phrase stick in your mind like a burr when unencumbered by fussy images, but the topics radio embraces are wider. You would not get any TV station risking half an hour in peak time a serious exposition of scientific ethics, Icelandic sagas or the medieval church. But all have made great radio.

Radio leads, though it is rarely recognized: it is still common to see some press fanfare about a TV documentary 'scoop' on a scientific or artistic subject, and to remember hearing all about it on Radio 4 six months before. Derek Cooper was first with the news of BSE; *From our Own Correspondent* warned us about the Indonesian meltdown of the late-nineties weeks ahead of any other mass medium.

This book is not a dispassionate analysis of the craft and the state of radio. This is a very personal medium, and it seems appropriate to celebrate it through the prism of a personal memoir. I have been a very small player in the BBC story, and always a hired hand with no power. But I happen to have had a ringside seat in many arenas — news, local radio, world service, religion, documentaries — through much of my adult life. All I want to do here is to convey something of how it has been to work with the nuts and bolts of this extraordinary medium, and to express also how much it has given to my own life, as a listener.

As to wider conclusions, I prefer to stick to the old radio nostrum that the listener is not a fool. Nor is the reader. With reference to their own knowledge and listening, readers can use this book to refine their own conclusions about how the medium grew up, how it has changed, what it conveys about the British character, what kind of people have made it great and what mistakes have gravely endangered it.

All I can tell you is what I have seen, and felt,

and done. If anyone remembers incidents or atmospheres differently they are free to argue over the details. But it is, above all, a personal account. And through all the frustrations, a love story.

1

The Miracle

From almost as far back into childhood as I can remember, I wanted to make a radio.

Not a radio *programme*: I had no notion of performing, or interviewing, or throwing my own voice through the grille. Moving from country to country, school to school, as a diplomat's child I had neither security nor space to think of myself as a performer. No, it was the machine itself I wanted to construct. A transistor radio! Just typing the words out now gives me a strange, almost occult thrill.

In the 1950s it was common to refer to them specifically as 'transistor radios', to differentiate them from the noble, heavy old creatures whose valves glowed red through walnut fretwork or mahogany sunbursts. These were well on the way out by the middle of the decade, but certainly during our three years in Britain between foreign postings my village school in Walberswick used an old valve radio, with magical and mysterious names like 'Hilversum' on the dial. We would gather round it weekly for *Music and Movement* ('Stretch . . . aaaand . . . rest!'). For a time, we also made a circle of deal chairs for a singalong programme put together by BBC Schools Radio and entitled *Rhythm and Melody*. I remember it because we learned 'D'ye ken John Peel',

5

and 'Loch Lomond', and a baffling song which went:

> *Farewell Manchester, noble town fare-weh-*
> *eel!*
> *In thy majesty every soul can dwell!*

The walnut valve radio made a convincing teacher: broad-based, establishment, solid, almost royal. The trannies of which I dreamed were quite different: subversive, portable, colourful, plastic, crying out to be tuned to lighter fare like the excitingly cool and risqué wavelength of Radio Luxembourg.

The first small personal transistor radios were made in the US in 1954, and arrived in Britain two years later, little chunky palm-sized gadgets as tantalizing and desirable to us as mobile phones became to children of the 1990s. They had real glamour, with their neat, light, sweetie-bright cases. Pastel-coloured trannies turned up in magazine fashion shoots, held to models' ears in a carefree fashion or taking pride of place on a picnic cloth. With your friendly little personal radio you could listen to music anywhere, any time; you could swing it around on its wrist-strap while it played. Or, even more hilarious to this yearning seven year old, you could hide it in your pocket so that voices would mysteriously come out of nowhere when you fiddled with the little knob. You could have Goons or newsreaders or orchestras in your shorts pocket. It was a sort of audible dolls' house: a universe in the palm of your hand.

I didn't have a tranny, and I longed for one. On half-forgotten beaches in the Far East when I was smaller I had listened to the rushing of the sea in conch shells, and harboured a secret fancy that at any minute the blood-rushing sound might resolve itself into a few bars of dance music or a crisp BBC announcement. Moreover, I had a hankering to go deeper into the mystery of it all, and peer under the bonnet of this exciting vehicle. Which is odd, because I was and remain manually and technically inept, and the dream of building a tranny with my own hands was always an imprudent one. Yet I was a sitting duck when, in the small-ads at the back of my favourite comic one day, among the Seebackroscopes and Whoopee Cushions and stinkbombs, I found an advertisement for a kit — costing around ten shillings and sixpence — which would enable you to make your own transistor radio. It would be, said the small print, 'a marvel, hardly bigger than a pack of cards'.

I nagged, I saved, I dedicated my birthday money and eventually sent off the postal order. Soon I would be holding music to my ear and conjuring deep distant voices from my pocket. Soon the miracle would come.

★ ★ ★

It came. I suppose one of the functions of mail order is to accustom the young early to the dismay and disappointment of adult life. What they sent was a plastic case in two parts, some little metal bits, and a mass of mystifying wires and knurled knobs, accompanied by a dispiriting sheet of paper with the kind of diagrams that make you want to cry just looking at them. I had never even made a successful Meccano model from a diagram.

My mother took one look at this messy boxful and detailed our live-in mother's help, Vera Wilson (known as Woose) to assist me. Woose was a dry, angular, entertaining but always mildly unpredictable presence. She had travelled with us to several foreign postings without herself changing one iota, and was worshipped by my small brothers. But my own most tightly defined and grateful memory of her concerns that week when together, night after night in the chilly boxroom, she and I tried to build the bloody little radio. We had to buy an electric soldering iron and a roll of fascinatingly bendy solder; I suspect that these cost rather more than the kit itself, but by this stage my mother was resigned to paying up.

Then we plunged into the instructions, trying to distinguish 'Busbar A' from 'Busbar B' without actually knowing quite what a busbar was. We peered, and dripped solder, and sucked our burned fingers, and wondered whether in doing so we had given ourselves lead poisoning. We poked wires through tiny holes and wrinkled our noses at the alien, laboratory smells of melted plastic and hot wire. I was particularly struck by the inside of the loudspeaker, which was about the size of the top of an ice-cream cone, and when I asked how it worked was vaguely told 'vibration'. My father was still in

Angola at the time, and my big brother at boarding school: we were a household of *distraite* women and small children, not at all fitted for an electronic challenge involving solder.

When each day's struggle had ended I went to bed and dreamed of the day when voices from far away would vibrate through the cone and the pierced plastic, emerging human and distinct from the mess of wires and clips and blobby solder. I knew that broadcasts hung all around us in the air, all the time, just waiting to be picked up; my mother had her big Roberts radio on for much of the time, and our family ritual whenever we were in England was to turn on the tinky-tonk music of *Listen with Mother* and — after the announcer said in a syrupy voice 'Are you sitting comfortably?' — to shout 'No!' before she went on to say: 'Then I'll begin'. And together we would rock with laughter at the Glums in *Take it from Here*, doing 'Oooh, Ron!' 'Yais, Eth?', and giggle over Jimmy Edwards' suggestive lines about only using the front room for important occasions 'Like Christmas, or Mrs Glum's All Over Wash'.

The entrancing thing about BBC comedy in the 1950s was its ingenuity in sneaking round the immortal Reithian guidelines laid out in the Variety Programmes Policy Guide of 1948. In the ironic spirit of today these have been republished in replica form to sell in the BBC shop, with their:

9

Absolute ban upon the following: —

Jokes about —
Lavatories
Effeminacy in men
Immorality of any kind

Suggestive references to —
Honeymoon couples
Chambermaids
Fig leaves
Prostitution
Ladies' underwear, e.g. winter draws on
Animal habits, e.g. rabbits
Lodgers
Commercial travellers . . .

You weren't allowed to say 'basket', to approve of drunkenness or to parody Biblical characters with the exception, mystifyingly, of Noah. Nor could you make jokes that:

might be taken to encourage: —
Strikes or industrial disputes
The Black Market
Spivs and Drones

We giggle at the restrictions now, but they were a marvellous stimulus to dirty creativity. Jules and Sandy eventually got through under the wire, magnificently effeminate men talking gay slang or 'polari' ('Ooh! Mr 'Orne! Lovely to vada your dolly old eek!'). So did the spivvy Sid James character in *Hancock*, and Mr Glum who was clearly both a spiv and a drone, and whose

10

entire mission was to avoid honest work of any kind. Post-Reithian prudery gave new impetus to surrealism, inventive euphemism, and that spirit of high jinks and danger which flourishes best when a stern, slightly humourless headmaster is only just out of earshot.

Anyway, it was tantalizing to know that the sounds which fed this big serious family radio were available, freely, to anybody whose busbars and blobs were correctly botched together. I itched for control of the big radio. Sometimes when Woose and I had given up for the evening I sneaked into the kitchen, pushed the short-wave button and twiddled the grubby white knob to pick up continental stations. It reassured me that there was a whole world out there which would make the fiddly wires and blobby solder wonderfully worthwhile. I wrote a poem while I waited, about a blind boy tuning a radio in the dark:

He heard the BBC
A calm collected voice
That kept cold sanity
And order in the place . . .

Then the boy twirls on, and stumbles into a zone of wilder broadcasts:

Music, laughter, leaping flames
Swedes and Swiss and wild DJs . . .

There was obviously bound to be danger in such deep magic. For a while I worried secretly about

11

whether there was any difference between radio waves and radioactivity, and considered the possibility that my new possession might gradually kill me. We were very nuclear-conscious, then: it was the height of the Cold War, and besides we had the Sizewell A nuclear power station being built a few miles north of us. Grownups muttered about radioactivity and made cryptic, doom-laden remarks about our luminous watch-dials. I also had a secret theory that if we wired the tranny up wrong it might summon tentacled aliens down to earth in a spaceship (*Quatermass and the Pit* was showing on the black-and-white television which we were allowed to watch down the lane at Mr Cleminson's). Yet despite all these misgivings about the magical device, I continued to long for it to come to life.

After a week of labour, it did. We put the battery in, switched on, moved the tuning knob and got a crackle. Many years later, in a BBC classroom, I was to identify such crackles as emanating from dirty contacts on a fader and requiring to be reported, on the correct fault form, to control room maintenance engineers. At seven years old I just bent over it with rapt attention, trying tiny adjustments, wondering where the crackle was being sent from. Then in a brief Eureka moment I found a skein of weak Morse code: my first signal from the sky.

And that was it. We never found any identifiable station, speech or music. Just the crackle and the moment of Morse. 'Marconi would have settled for that, on a first try,' said my mother philosophically, and we put the useless thing away in a drawer.

★ ★ ★

She was, of course, right. In her generation broadcast radio had been the brand-new miracle that the Internet became in the 1990s. She would have been three or four when the Marconi company got its licence to send out experimental transmissions of music and speech from Chelmsford, and launched itself with a concert by Dame Nellie Melba. It was dangerous voodoo then: transmissions were banned for a year by the Post Office after the armed forces complained to government that a concert by the tenor Lauritz Melchior had interfered with aircraft communications frequencies. But by the time my mother was at school, in 1922, radio had begun again, with 2LO and Writtle both on the air — though unpublicized — and the brisk, flippant, pre-BBC tones of Captain Peter Eckersley chirping: 'This is two Emma Toc WRITTLE testing, two Emma Toc WRITTLE testing, hello, hello.' And in 1922 the British Broadcasting Company — not yet a corporation — opened a proper service, under the leadership of a dour and driven Scottish engineering manager called John Reith.

In those days too there was much building of homemade radios, by methods immortally described by Peter Black in his light-hearted 1972 history of the BBC *The Biggest Aspidistra in the World*. He remembers putting his metal wire, the 'cat's whisker', in contact with a lump of crystal and connecting prized headphones to it. After consulting the *Wireless Constructor* magazine he learnt to use a pound of no. 16 DCC wire, a sixpenny crystal, a piece of dry wood, some tinfoil and a hexagonal pickle bottle to wind the wire round, and get 2LO. To get Chelmsford you needed a tonic elixir bottle. There was a lot of fuss about oscillation, caused by people having their coils too close together, and according to Black the broadcasters often put out stern warnings to residents in certain streets to stop causing interference to their neighbours. It was an inventive, innocent, optimistic, Pooterish activity.

My mother remembers that her father made a 2LO crystal set, and switched it on sometime in 1922. There was a dead silence. 'We all sat round the kitchen table in the silence, and despaired.' But it was only a breakdown in transmission that day, and soon the crystal sprang to life. Inspired, that grandfather I never knew constructed a proper valve set in a home-made cabinet. No wonder my mother didn't mind paying for the soldering iron; she must have thought that the radio-building gene had skipped a generation.

Reading since then the histories of broadcasting, I have found to my delight that the pioneers of the BBC were every bit as romantic about the new medium as any secretive seven year old. John Reith himself was of that bracing Aberdonian type which longs to do good to others, especially moral good. His deputy, Captain C. A. Lewis was of the same mind, and much in love with the technical miracle. He wrote how wonderful it was that in this twentieth century great music could be carried 'along the roadsides, over the hills, through towns, brushed by trees, soaked by rain, swayed by gales'. He marvelled at the notion that:

the shepherd on the downs, the lonely crofter in the farthest Hebrides, and what is more important the labourer in his squalid tenement, equally the lonely invalid on her monotonous couch, may all in spirit sit side by side with the patrons of the stalls and hear some of the best performances in the world.

They broadcast *The Magic Flute* in 1923 live from Covent Garden. But the Savoy Orpheans and other light dance-bands were also staple fare from the very start; so the labourer and the lonely invalid could equally sit side by side with the cocktail set at the Savoy.

If the rhetoric sometimes got out of hand, and the sense of responsibility extended (as it did, under Reith) to banning divorced singers from performing on the pure BBC airwaves, there is some excuse. These men were presiding over a revolution, faster and more dramatic and cheaper to the consumer than Caxton's first printing-press. With astonishing rapidity (*vide* my grandfather building his cabinet) radios became the heart of the home. Peter Black

15

quotes a wonderful advertisement for lamp-shades which illustrates this better than anything else could:

> Women of Britain! The radio has undoubtedly helped to keep your husband and boys away from the club and kept them at home where they thus experience the benefits of your gentle charm and influence; but you must now go one step further and make your home comfy and cheerful by having Hailglass Shades and Globes on your lights. Your menfolk, as they listen to the radio in a home made bright and comfy by our charmingly coloured glassware, will indeed feel that they are in a real Heaven on Earth.

Other advertisements of the period catch the same tone; women knitting by the grille of the radio, children at their feet, tame menfolk sucking on their pipes as they listen together to John Henry or A. J. Alan.

I dwell on the early pioneers, working decades before I was born, because there is — to this day — something inspiring in their unquestioning belief that broadcasting was a wonderful and democratic way to share the best things, the best ideas and words and music, with all their fellow citizens irrespective of social position or wealth. Reith believed that his duty was to offer the public 'something better than it ever thought it wanted'. In the *1929 BBC Handbook* the section on music says:

Broadcasting, that magical agent, has made available by means of comparatively simple apparatus and at next to no cost the finest things there are to hear . . . literally millions of people have heard for the first time in their lives the simple, youthful and sparkling tunes of Papa Haydn or the elegant Mozart and the joyful early quartets of Beethoven and realized that therein lies a wealth of melody undreamed of. Hosts of bright, impressionable children whose music had consisted mainly of snatches of music hall ditties inflicted by itinerant executants in the bar entrance, or sobs of the worst type of sentimental slop played in the local cinema . . . have heard over the broadcast such music as must have had a great and good influence on the sensitive unfolding mind.

Peter Black, quoting this, says mischievously that the early Reithians' desire to do the nation good 'gleams, as a beam of light strikes a domed forehead'. Certainly it led to plenty of absurdities, from the ban on divorcees to the worry about lodger-jokes; and yet there was something noble about that early vision. The first pioneers wanted to share. Moreover, they wanted to share as widely as possible, not to exclude, patronize, or seize the medium as a plaything for the already cultured classes. They were enthusiasts for social inclusion, seventy years before the phrase was coined. 'BBC English' is often sneered at, but in their use of language the pioneers were extraordinarily careful to find words and expressions which, while not vulgar, were easily accessible to the whole population.

'Unaffected simplicity of utterance alone gets over,' said Reith. These were the men who grabbed George Bernard Shaw and invited him to 'do anything' for a nugatory fee, and this was the medium which made Shaw agree, and come into the studio to read 'O'Flaherty, VC' for no fee at all. Radio began in this intense excitement, the same excitement that infected me as a small child forty years later, in a Suffolk boxroom, struggling with my busbars and longing to join in.

Radio's simplicity and universality was, and remains, magical. That its early years in Britain should have fallen under the care of men who considered themselves to be warriors for truth and goodness is a lucky chance. They believed (and carved eventually over their lintel) that broadcasting was there to relay, in the Pauline phrase, 'whatsoever things are pure, lovely and of good report'. They hoped that radio would make the world better. Reith — a cussed, lonely creature himself — wrote in *Broadcast over Britain:* 'It has been said that there are two kinds of loneliness: insulation in space and isolation of spirit. These are both dispelled by wireless.'

And when Captain Lewis walked home late on summer evenings after a bracing day of broadcasting in the 1920s he saw the evidence of radio's benevolent influence in every back garden: 'The aerial posts standing, like spears against the sky'.

A romantic, knightly vision: gentle and good, gallant and bold. Radio was to fall a long way short of all these ideals at times. But at least it had them. Its beginnings were noble.

2

Pirates and Patriarchs

I got my tranny in the end. I think my father brought it home from one of his journeys. I remember the set vividly: it was slightly bigger than a pack of cards, a pale-green box encased in a brown leather case with holes pierced over the loudspeaker to let the sound out, a detail which I thought very sophisticated. While I was writing this I noticed that in a drawer in this house, four decades later, I seem to have a very similar modern set, disregarded and devoid of wonder. It must have been bought in haste for a tenner or so, on some trip away from home, and shoved in a drawer when it came out of the overnight bag.

Handling it, I try to recapture the wonder with which I approached the original. Impossible. These days it is just another radio, and radios are two-a-penny, like taps or electric lights. You feel quite irritated if there isn't one in the room with you, to switch on whenever you want.

But I do remember the tent in the garden where, on summer nights, we were allowed to sleep. The little radio played there, late into the night under the drooping orange ridge, tuned to the pop Radio Luxembourg. Certain tunes endure, mystifyingly, in my head: I know about 'Che Sera Sera', but was there really a song which went 'I'll take my Suki Yaki back to

20

Nagasaki'? Like all cheap sets down the ages, that first tranny was rather better at catching pop stations than the Home Service. It is something to do with a more limited and aggressive dynamic range in pop records and DJ patter. Rational speech, in broadcast physics as in general debate, makes a weaker signal.

But I was very happy with it. It linked me to the world. It gave me music on tap long before Sony Walkmen or even the ground-breaking Dansette portable record-player, which arrived with the 1960s. Watching my own children zapping idly through satellite TV channels or conjuring up music on tiny digital and minidisc players, I have to restrain myself from sentences beginning 'In my day . . . ', but cannot stifle a small, treacherous regret that they have never had that buzz, that mystery. I suppose it is replaced for the present generation by the ability to download music off the Internet.

Back indoors, in the long Suffolk winter, I would listen under the bedclothes in defiance of house rules. I would stretch my small ear uncomfortably with the single white plastic earphone, a nasty medical-looking device, and fiddle experimentally with the dial. 'Suki Yaki' and Radio Lux were only the start: I roamed on, ever further. There was BBC World Service, with Big Ben and the high, tinny crashing of 'Imperial Echoes' launching *Radio Newsreel* (and fore-shadowing my first job, had I but known it). There were jabbering French and Dutch voices, and high, thin music which I always thought must come from Norway because it sounded like

21

snow. Also, at that time, the isolated Albanian regime was putting out a powerful MF signal, with a distinctive chiming fanfare, after which a stern Iron Curtain woman would read in English a news bulletin of such extraordinary dullness that sleep followed immediately. '*The — Central — Committee — has — announced — that — the — national — plan — for — agricultural — production — has — been — ex — ceeded.*' The signal was a devil to hold: I would wake to a hard uncomfortable earphone lump pressing into my head and a faint shashing, as if the sea had swallowed Albania like Atlantis.

I loved that little box in its leather case. I wish I could remember when, and in what country, I eventually lost it.

It could be anywhere. After the Suffolk interlude our travelling family life resumed. I have written about that wandering childhood elsewhere, so will only pick out the moments when radio again sparked its magic. In northern France, we could just about get BBC long-wave, but in those days that confined us to the Light Programme (now Radio 2). My mother listened to the saccharine choruses of *Sing Something Simple* and to *Friday Night is Music Night*, and *Woman's Hour* was on long-wave until the late-1960s; but there was little in any of it for us four children. In France, and later in the decorous boredom of Switzerland, we were more likely to work the old record-player to death, playing again and again our family LPs (Danny Kaye, Tom Lehrer, Vaughan Williams' 'Fantasia on Greensleeves') and precious hoarded singles of our own generation's newborn rock.

Recorded speech, however, had an equally powerful pull: the few speech LPs on the family shelf constantly intrigued me. In an eclectic Anglo-American mix we had radio comedies from the Goons to Bob Newhart; later there was a spoof on the family life of the Kennedys, *The First Family*, which would probably be a collector's item if any of us could remember who had it last. There was a recording of 'Peter and the Wolf'; there was Yehudi Menuhin's introduction to the instruments of the orchestra (I did love the piccolo). And there was a dramatization, in French, of the trial of Joan of Arc, with much emphasis on her maintenance of '*ma pudeur*', to which I resorted in every maudlin and self-pitying mood from the age of ten to about fifteen. ('*Si j'y suis — que Dieu m'y garde! Si j'y suis pas — que Dieu m'y mette!*') I was, I suppose, learning a bit about radio drama. Certainly I was always at my happiest when taking in amusement or edification either through reading or listening. The cinema held a second rank. Maybe it is an effect of being short-sighted, hating wearing specs and being secretly convinced that I would go blind. The world of sound, of tones of voice and subtleties of atmosphere, was a world where I was everybody's equal.

In between European posts there was a brutal interlude in Johannesburg. For the second part of that disturbing year I did my lessons alone, at home. SABC radio was not particularly interesting, except for a short feature which seemed to

23

run every day, entitled *Death Touched My Shoulder* (you have to say it in a heavy Afrikaans accent to get the effect). It was about people — white people, obviously, this was 1963 — who had had narrow escapes from death. I found it utterly riveting: one simple voice told a frightening story, allowing the imagination to riot undisturbed over cliff-edges, tottering buildings, runaway machinery, hot lion breath or whatever. Years later and continents away I sometimes wake from a nightmare and identify it without hesitation or difficulty as having its roots in *Death Touched My Shoulder*.

★ ★ ★

During those years, from 1959 to 1964, I more or less lost touch with UK radio. By the time I was back at boarding-school in Kent, aged fourteen, a great deal had changed. For one thing, radio had completely lost its primacy. In the mid-fifties, when I left, not everyone had television, and what there was was strictly monochrome and therefore much less compelling. People forget that, before colour and big, high-quality screens, TV had to seize the audience's attention with words, almost as urgently as radio did. That is why old TV drama seems quaintly verbose now. When I was small we didn't have a set at home. By the time we were coming home to Suffolk for summer holidays five years later, we had a TV in the living room as a matter of course, and nobody questioned that the main flow of popular culture

24

was through the small screen.

Once back in Britain and in the TV age, like everyone else, we became familiar with Fyfe Robertson's big white beard and Cliff Michelmore saying 'The next Tonight will be tomorrow night'; with TW3, Z Cars, Cathy Come Home and Ena Sharples' hairnet down at the Rover's Return. Meanwhile on the radio *Life with the Lyons, Take it from Here* and *The Goons* seemed to have gone, but *Just a Minute* still dominated Sunday lunchtime, and to complement the News (which my father would never miss) there was *Round the Horne*, with jokes of extraordinary, blessed filthiness beneath the booming bonhomie. And there was the eternal *Archers*, even duller then; and dreary High Anglican Sunday services with a lot of chanted psalms, and classic plays suitable for doing the ironing to on wet afternoons, and pat little detective dramas which always seemed to begin:

> *(Rat-at-tat-tat!)*
> *'Come in — Oh! Officer! Is there . . . ?'*
> *'Mrs Finch? Shagbrugh police. I'm very*
> *sorry. There's been an accident . . . '*

If you were a teenager, however, the most notable thing about BBC Radio in the sixties was that it was not at all cool. Every self-respecting tranny was determinedly tuned to the pop pirates, which were chaotic and funny and silly and illegal and generally irresistible. Nobody of my generation can hear the song *'Caroline! Ay-ay-ay-ay, she really is fi-yeen!'* without a nostalgic twinge. I can still sing the old Radio London jingle, too, and once or twice in my A-level term, summer 1967, I picked up 'Swinging Radio England' from yet another ship. At school in Tunbridge Wells it was also possible, at times, to get Screaming Lord Sutch's brainchild 'Radio City, The Tower of Power' from the Shivering Sands Fort nine miles off Whitstable in the Thames Estuary.

It is worth paying tribute to the pirate stations, brief though their heyday was. Between the heady rebel days of 1964 and the spoilsport Marine Etc (Broadcasting) Offences Bill of 1967, they made an incalculable difference to the course of British radio broadcasting.

For BBC Radio, frankly, had gone soggy. On the face of it, things were the same as ever. The Home Service continued to fulfil its remit — providing decent plays, features, news, discussions and 'talks'. Slightly to my shame, when I was fifteen, heavily urged on by my mother I submitted and recorded a 'talk' on *Woman's Hour* myself, about being a globe-trotting diplomatic service child and going to foreign schools. It was pretty awful, but then all of the Home Service at that time felt a bit staid: overscripted, twee and tweedy. The Reithian energy had run out of steam but Reithian strictness still hung on. The best thing to be said about the 1960s Home Service is that even then its comedy and panel games were so inventive they always got snapped up by TV. But otherwise, if you look at the schedules of the time, they breathe an air of weary late-middle age: *Gardeners' Question Time, Talking About Antiques*, yet another production of *The Winslow Boy*, Freddie Grisewood ensuring that *Any Questions* stayed respectable and uncontentious, anodyne little interviews on *Home This Afternoon*, and the execrable *Petticoat Line*, in which Renee Houston, Anona Winn et al were expected to give a 'woman's view' on issues of the day, posing variously as two-dimensional female caricatures of vamp, giggler or harridan.

The Third Programme did a workmanlike job, with classical music and academic talks and a select but devoted audience. The Light Programme, on the other hand, was ludicrously out of date. As the sixties revolution of youth culture and music unrolled, the BBC shrank away from it in maidenly horror, like a comedy spinster leaping on a chair to avoid a mouse. It also shrank from any idea that the sacred medium could ever be commercial (Lord Reith robustly compared commercial radio to 'dog-racing, smallpox and the Bubonic Plague'). Fine: but the BBC simply would not provide what the public plainly wanted. It left pop broadcasting to the alien Radio Luxembourg, which in turn was in thrall to the big four record companies and thus no help to the smaller independent artists who were bursting with creativity and mischief. The Light Programme, which should have been embracing the up-and-coming music, remained staid, dated and safe — no place for the airing of new groups and the new beat.

Looking back, it is clear that by letting this happen and creating an ideal opening for the pirates, the BBC was frankly betraying its roots and its mission of universality. Reith and his early pioneers were by no means resistant to the swinging new music of their own age, and gave the dance bands a great deal of airtime and appreciation. They put out opera and symphonies but even Reith himself warned that 'Grand music will not do for everybody, every day'. Since his time, however, the Corporation itself had become vast and hierarchical and correspondingly sluggish. It frustrated and ignored the teenagers and twenties who were gladly paying six shillings and eightpence a time for the new singles, and went on feeding them their parents' music.

So the pirates came. Ronan O'Rahilly, the entrepreneur who started Radio Caroline on an old Danish ferry anchored off Frinton, said, 'Youth was busting out all over, there was a lot of money to be made. Things were really beginning to happen, and for the first time since the First World War Britain was swinging.' He named his station after Caroline Kennedy, the American President's daughter, after seeing a picture of her looking: 'So young, so fresh and happy. Exactly the feeling I wanted to get across on the air.'

The offshore pirates, half a dozen of them coming and going through three tense years of standoffs, litigation, raids and general governmental huffing, demonstrated to the wondering UK a new way to use radio. They challenged the BBC's self-imposed limits; they advertised, they ad-libbed, they were irreverent and spontaneous, they wooed their audience, they put untried, larky characters on the air. They enjoyed the technical miracle but treated it as a toy, not a sacrament. In a sense the mood they conveyed went all the way back to Captain Eckersley's jokes from Writtle and the first high-spirited impromptu broadcasts from 2LO. Like the early pioneers of radio they worked all hours, under improvised and chaotic conditions, forever going off the air due to technical glitches exacerbated by the rolling of the vessel which caused many a DJ to throw up between records, and many a needle to jump a groove or two when a big wave hit.

It was entrancing to listen to. At the most conservative estimate between ten and fifteen million listeners — by no means all teenagers — tuned in to the all-day pop and patter. The Postmaster-General, Anthony Wedgwood Benn, was in a quandary as pressure grew to make this maverick form of broadcasting part of national life forever by licensing onshore commercial radio. At a 1965 by-election Patrick Gordon Walker lost his safe Labour seat, dropping an 8,000 majority in Leyton, after a pressure group campaign put up posters saying 'Don't vote Labour, they are going to kill Caroline.' The *Sunday Express* suggested that all the fuss could be averted:

Radio Caroline and the others provide lively and gay music that millions of people want to hear.

Why, then, does not the BBC turn over

the Light Programme to just this kind of entertainment instead of the pompous, pretentious pap it so often now purveys?

There was also — even then — pressure to put advertising on the BBC Light Programme and thus make it a clone of the pirates. Asked about this, the Postmaster-General replied, 'It is tempting to deny but by denying you tend to confirm what you don't deny, and then by confirming and denying what you have announced before you have decided.' Oratorically, it was not Mr Benn's finest hour.

Meanwhile, pressure also mounted for local commercial radio, with an Association formed in 1964. The forty-year monopoly was beginning to look unsustainable. The BBC stirred uneasily, and began to form its own plans for local stations, putting out a pamphlet in 1966 to cheer up the beleaguered Postmaster-General. The pamphlet reiterated the traditional Corporation opposition to day-long pop, even if the public did seem to want it. BBC stations would never, said the pamphlet, be 'amplified juke boxes of the kind familiar to people who have travelled to some overseas countries'. Writing about this, the historian of the pirates Paul Harris says angrily that it was:

> . . . typical of the pompous, smug, tyrannical, you'll enjoy-what-you-get attitude of the BBC, which is financially supported by the British people who had no choice but to listen to its output until the pirate radio

stations came along and gave them what they wanted.

Reading that 1960s' blast of fury now, in conjunction with the early BBC pioneers' ideal of giving people 'something better than they think they want', I am struck by how difficult it has always been to strike a reasonable balance between a mission to educate and the perils of paternalism. It is perfectly true that BBC idealism brought wonderful music, mind-stretching talks and great drama to people who never knew they wanted such things. It was, in its time, a perfect complement to the high seriousness but genuine popularity of the Workers' Educational Association. But it is equally true that Auntie's tendency to sluggish pomposity has more than once almost been the death of her.

This also, paradoxically, explains much about the current twitchy populism in the television service as it rushes to meet the most thoughtless, rootless popular taste with gim-micky game shows and docusoaps. Like a recovering addict, the BBC fears that if it once tries to inspire and educate, it will not be able to stop itself and will end up as a despised schoolmarm with no friends. Like an alcoholic in recovery who cannot afford to remember how good claret once tasted but harps on about the degradation and hangovers, the BBC remembers none of the nobility or idealism of its early founders but only their absurdities. It would be good if one day the television service felt able to

31

relax, and accept its roots, and get over its hidden dread of being a bore. Sure, Lord Reith banned divorcees from the airwaves; sure, he compared commercial radio to the Bubonic Plague. But he also set the bands playing, the comedy roaring, and opened a thousand doors for a million people.

BBC Radio runs on a different cycle, and the risks are different. Although as I write Radio 1 is taking the populist route and rolling over to flash its pierced belly-button at the silliest extremes of youth culture, with Sara Cox devoting the sunrise hours to asking poor sleepy lorry-drivers from Solihull how big their willies are, by and large in radio the temptations of dumbing down are less than the opposite risk, of pomposity. In the sixties what seems to have happened is that the adventurers, the innovators, the challengers of the establishment and the cheerful populists, all went to television under Sir Hugh Greene's iconoclastic leadership and gave the nation TW3 and The Frost Report and Tonight and gritty kitchen-sink dramas. Therefore — on the old principle that the emigrants are the best and strongest — rather too many nostalgic and timid souls stayed in radio. Certainly the Corporation's response to the pirate radio stations was curiously depressing in tone. Stuart Hood, in the mid-sixties, wrote in *Encounter* that:

The parallel with the Corporation's attitude when Independent Television came into existence will be certainly inescapable — the same moral indignation, the same incredulity that the public might not wish to have an undiluted diet of BBC programmes.

And Kenny Everett, then a pirate DJ, compared the style of the pirates to that of poor old Auntie:

Our ad-libbing, as opposed to the BBC's scripted rubbish, sounds fantastic . . . after all the stilted gob which is scripted by the BBC it sounds quite human . . . we are radio, they are . . . something diabolical. Commercial radio on land would be a boot up the arse for the BBC . . . non-competitive, staid and aunty-ish.

The pirates did not get their onshore berth. The BBC accepted that it would have to heave itself into the second half of the century. Gradually the net closed on the seasick ravers with their swaying turntables and blinking generators; and in the heart of London W1, close to All Souls Church and the sacred premises of Broadcasting House, Radio 1 opened in 1967.

It had the sense to know that its only hope was to employ many of the pirates' old DJs. The new station was not, as the *Sunday Express* had proposed, a substitute for the Light Programme. That survived as Radio 2; which, as it turned out, was just as well for Radio 1 DJs like Ed Stewart, Terry Wogan, Pete Murray, Jimmy Young, Johnnie Walker, etc, who found that as they became too ludicrously mature for Radio 1 they had somewhere to pass their declining years. And meanwhile the BBC went ahead with a pilot project of nine local radio stations on VHF, which were not, repeat not, to be 'amplified juke boxes' or to carry advertising. Corporation statements were very firm on that point.

⋆ ⋆ ⋆

This is where I come in, with my tranny. You could not be a 1960s teenager, however timid and square, without being aware of the battle between the pirates and Auntie. For me the issue revived my old fascination with the medium of radio itself. Once I got to the sixth form a fresh impetus to listen was provided by a much improved *Today* programme, which had updated itself by teaming the old-style brainless bonhomie of Jack de Manio with an equally jovial but rather more solid former court correspondent, John Timpson. It was Timpson's voice, booming and harrumphing from the school bathrooms in the morning which caused a short-lived ban on radios being taken in there. It was not, one of our nunly guardians felt, at all suitable for a deep male voice to resonate round a room where a modest young girl might be unclothed. I used to love telling John Timpson this in after years; and oh, how he loved to hear it and to know how much of a sexual threat he could be, even over the airwaves.

Listening to *Today* got even better when de Manio bumbled off and Robert Robinson joined

Timpson. I was at university by then, and addicted to Radio 4 in the morning. I liked the jokes and the vague sense of being in the swim of current events, even if I understood little of them. And when you are alone but adult, far from family, pretty broke and altogether uncertain of your future in the world, that is the time that speech radio has its best chance of capturing you entirely.

I still listened to the Top Twenty, but Radio 4 was my audio drug of choice. TV, remember, was still mainly monochrome and not a great part of student life. Only a very few programmes brought us together in pub or common-room: Monty Python was the main one, although there was always a certain kind of student who remained spookily addicted to The Magic Roundabout. In the holidays, in Suffolk, the main use of TV was for late-night satire, or to while away wet afternoons with Bette Davis melodramas, or old war films like *Above Us the Waves*, *The Cruel Sea* and *The Way to the Stars*.

Gradually, privately, I decided what I wanted to do. Dreams of acting fell away, and so did thoughts of publishing or advertising (the standard destination for Eng Lit graduates). As for research, although I dutifully prepared a topic for a D.Litt I never seriously wanted to stay in academe either. I wanted to go into radio. It was not, curiously, a showbiz urge: I just wanted to be among microphones and tapes and transmitters. I had unfinished business with those busbars A and B.

In my last year, the chance came. The BBC was expanding its chain of local radio stations, another effect of the rude kick up the fundament it had received from the pirates. After the first eight were successful, a second generation of twelve was commissioned, the fourth of which was Oxford. It went on the air on 29 October, 1970, on VHF and medium-wave; its twenty staff settled two storeys above a car showroom in Summertown, a mile or so north of what Oxford students consider the limits of the civilized world.

It was emphatically a town, rather than gown, station, concerned more with the Leyland plant at Cowley than with Balliol and Corpus Christi. However, they put an advertisement in the Daily Information sheet, asking for students who might want to help make a fifteen-minute weekly programme called *About the University*. Before the day was out I was up there, in stark defiance of my tutor (it was my finals year). I went with a group of fellow-volunteers, climbed up two flights of concrete stairs and went through the swing doors of my first radio station.

And — possibly because I had watched just one too many of those black-and-white war films — the moment I saw the words 'Ops Room' on a door and caught a glimpse of enchantingly 1940s telephone exchange-type headphones and a jackfield of plugs beyond, I was lost.

3

Violet Elizabeth Gets a Platform

It was much later that I got to know the realities of local radio in general, and Radio Oxford in particular. As a student my main contact was with the long-suffering veteran producer who was put in charge of us, Michael Henderson. He had joined the BBC after the war, taken a long break and second career in social work, and returned to spend his pre-retirement years helping the young team at Oxford to settle in. He had crinkly grey hair, a limp, and a faintly donnish air which made us students feel quite at home. On the other hand, his very presence was a firm indication to us that BBC stations were not going to be wild, miniature versions of the dear departed pirate-ships. They were going to be somewhere halfway between Radios 4 and 2, with added local earnestness.

I liked Mike. He represented my first sighting of the species — fairly common then, nearly extinct now — which we may call Old BBC. In the years to come I was to learn to spot the type a mile off, whether it manifested itself as a World Service announcer or a backroom operations manager: decent, painstaking, honest, dignified, patriarchally kind, not noted for an obvious sense of humour yet possessing a curious, unsettling, frilly edge of fey imagination. 'A

37

traditional BBC man,' I was once told, 'is basically a civil servant with a secret spangled tutu worn under his suit.'

Mike, to do him justice, had a particularly strong streak of whimsy. It surfaced first when he presented to us — the Rolling Stones generation — his idea of a signature tune for the programme. It was a cheerful little ditty rather in the style of Sandy Wilson's *Salad Days* (which at the time was not yet ripe for ironic revival but dead as the dodo). It was sung, in a pleasing tenor, by himself and began:

> *What do you know-oo* — *about the Uni-*
>   *versitee?*
> *Where can you go-ooh* — *about the Uni-*
>   *versitee . . . ?*

Our faces said it all. Before long, he binned it.

★　★　★

We worked in groups of five, earnestly cobbling together a fourteen-minute programme every third week with 'University News' and rather inept interviews. The real staff were a shade aloof. They were exalted by their new possession of this pocket radio-station, this broadcasting dolls'-house with all its shiny new equipment. They did not particularly want to share it with a bunch of students. Under Mike's infinitely patient tutelage, though, we learned how to record interviews on portables — great heavy Uher 4000s, weighing half a stone — and occasionally in the studio. We were briefly instructed in how to hold a microphone steady without causing dreadful cracklings from its wire, and how to edit brown quarter-inch tape on the big Studer machines with a blade and chinagraph.

Editing entranced me: it was so pleasingly basic and mechanical. You wobbled the length of tape to and fro against the head, playing the sound off it in slow-motion, then found and marked the gaps or clicks or 'errr's or rustles you needed to nip out, hedged them in with yellow chinagraph marks, and sliced them out with a razor blade. Or else, even more exciting, you used the hard edge of a consonant in a fluffed sentence to mark and cut to the hard edge of the same word's retake, leaving the mistake curled up discarded on the carpet. We learned how to slice cleanly along the diagonal in the block with a fresh razor blade, and how to ease the two cut ends together and fuse them with white sticky tape. We worked with painful slowness; late at night Mike would yawn patiently, hoping to go home, gathering up his files and tapes with a clatter at the far end of the Ops Room while we frowned and pecked and struggled with our miserable little bits of the Warden of Wadham or Librarian of All Souls.

For some of the student broadcasters, interest waned very fast and they never came back. Me, I was in paradise. This was it, it was real, it was radio, I was learning the grammar of it from the very bottom. Granted, our programme was pretty dull and nobody was listening at that stage. But it was a start.

★ ★ ★

After finals, I had to stay on in the enervating heat of midsummer Oxford to clear up and hand back the house I had shared with vanished compeers. I drew this short straw because I also had a summons to a viva voce exam at the end of July. There was a clear month to kill, and no money left for anything but the boiled rice and grated cheese which form the staple of a student's end-of-term provisioning. I sold my scholar's gown and my big dictionary, and gratefully accepted my tutor's offer of £25 to catalogue her private library. I do not think Mrs Bednarowska really wanted it cataloguing, but she kept up the pretence, sat elegantly frowning over exam papers and put up with frequent confused cries from her study along the lines of: 'Do you want Machiavelli classified as a Foreigner or an Influence?' or 'Do you reckon *Mandeville's Travels* should be fiction or non-fiction?'

Funded by this morning job, I biked up to Summertown and offered to devote my afternoons to the service of Radio Oxford. I was prepared to wash the floors, if they had asked me to. Instead, the programme organizer Owen Bentley sat me down and proposed that I should make them a daily — *daily!* — five-minute slot on tourist attractions, entitled *Tourist Trap*.

'Our thinking,' he said grandly, 'is that

Americans are in the habit of always tuning to the local VHF station wherever they are. So when they come to Oxford they will tune to us automatically, and we will be ready for them with *Tourist Trap.*' There would be no fee as such, he explained, but a princely budget of £5 per programme, which could be spent as we wished.

Given that the BBC's mission statement for these stations laid heavy emphasis on service and relevance to the local community, it would seem that Owen's vision of serving American tourists was a maverick one: a glimpse, perhaps, of the mad spangled tutu beneath his corporate suit. But that was BBC local radio in the early days: deeply, pleasingly eccentric. If someone had an idea, especially if it cost nothing, they had only to nag the station manager for five minutes and it was in production. I was to learn the full gamut of local radio weirdness in the next few years, but on that day I merely nodded with unquestioning enthusiasm, asked with awe whether I really got to borrow a Uher to do my reports with, and skipped gleefully down past the car showroom, walking on air.

I knew my limitations, and accepted that I desperately needed a partner in this enterprise. It was a tricky call. Everyone I knew was either long departed from the city, or else so dreadfully cool and hip and stoned that the idea of doing a tourist show on local radio would probably kill them. By great good fortune I ran into a graduate who owned a car and found himself at a loose end that July. He was a tousle-haired, cheerful chap, a dead ringer for anyone's idea of *Just William*; he had been reading Japanese, and was therefore theoretically a bit of an expert on tourists as well. Best of all, he planned to work for the BBC. His name was William Horsley: you have heard him a hundred times, as one of the most distinguished correspondents in Japan and elsewhere, a serious and intellectual reporter.

These qualities were not, I fear, fully stretched in our panicky and chaotic production of *Tourist Trap*. We had to do five per week, and set ourselves ambitious targets, like a general programme on the chimes of college clocks, which was the most labour-intensive horror to collect; we banged on church doors, made desperate phone calls from callboxes, running out of tuppences in the middle of our pitch, and were the bane of museum curators from Pitt-Rivers to the Ashmolean. We edited whenever we were allowed near the radio station kit, and lived in terror of breaking some of it. We fantasized a little about being cutting-edge red-hot journalists getting scoops, but were pathetically grateful for any halfway coherent vicar with a mildly interesting story about his church steeple.

Somehow we got our programmes made. A month later, on a family holiday, I wrote a piece for the *Punch* student journalist competition (subject 'What I did in the hols') and offer this excerpt, because it sums up some of the excited panic of those hot days:

★　★　★

Some days five minutes felt like a mere second; others an aching void, five minutes to be padded out with Hello and Welcomes, with Over Now To Williams, and Victorian musical boxes. We interviewed curators, vicars, architects and archaeologists; sometimes we sat for hours beneath towers that wouldn't strike or couldn't strike or turned out to be closed for cleaning; sometimes we heaved a tape recorder up spiral staircases to speak with unsimulated breathlessness of the view from the rain-lashed summit; five minutes a day. And yet we dreamed . . .

It's Spurve, Bill Spurve, the man from Record-a-vicar, speeding in now at the wheel of the fast bike, spooling the tape on with one deft flick of the forefinger . . .

And we dreamed in the studio, too. Late at night once we sat, William and I, ankle-deep in magnetic tape cuttings, elbows skilfully spliced to the chairs with mysteriously unwound sticky tape, breathing heavily as we removed the stammers from an elderly Preservationist's 3 minutes 43 of magnetized erudition; and a buzzer sounded on the switchboard next to us. A disembodied voice said, 'Hello, Ops Room?'

'Hello,' I said wildly, stopping the Preservationist with a trembling forefinger. William ran from the room to fetch an expert. The voice returned, impatient. 'Ops Room, Ops Room, are you receiving me?'

Old war films blurred across the plastic switchboard. Impotent, trapped in the sinking submarine, the radio out of order, I listened to the searching, beseeching voice. 'Ops Room, Ops

Room . . . ' A shark swam past the window in the gloom. Suddenly William came back with a young man, dark and intent and called (he just had to be) Nigel. Nigel pressed an unlabelled talkback button and snapped, 'Ops Room to Radio Car, over.'

After he had gone, we looked at each other and I think it was me who finally said, '*I* want to say, 'Ops Room to Radio Car. Over'.'

'With *earphones* on!'

'And bombs falling, a couple of miles away, on some mother's son.'

We switched our tape on again and moodily removed ten seconds on the West Face and its history.

★　★　★

Reading it again I am struck — apart from the war-film fantasy — by the stress on the mechanical and electrical aspect of the task. Remember that I was, after all, just an Eng Lit graduate, and had not even done Physics O-level. I had only just found out that what made sounds reproducible was, in those pre-digital days, no more or less than the realignment of teeny-weeny magnetic particles on the very surface of the plastic-backed tape. I was thrilled by the very idea. And when we found ourselves elegantly fading sound effects, easing snatches of music between our interviewees' words, or capturing the lovely whirr and clunk of some clock in the Museum of the History of Science or the dry rattle of a primitive

44

instrument in the Pitt-Rivers, the sheer magic of carrying home an atmospheric moment on millions of little magnetic dingbats was so exciting that it made us hop and grin and chortle. It even enabled William to put up very gracefully with a partnership in which, I see with hindsight, I must have done a fair impression of Violet Elizabeth Bott.

★　★　★

I knew where I was going, now. The BBC had done its routine trawl of the universities at the end of the year, and I picked up a handout — I still have it, with the 1960s logo and a red stripe along the top — about the job of Programme Operations Assistant. The BBC, it said in lordly tones, required a number of men and women between twenty and twenty-five to train as POAs.

Everything in the BBC in those days was a string of initials, whether it was a human being, a programme or a bit of kit: it was a bit like the army. POAs, DOAs, TOs, PAs, PPMs, TD7s, QCRs, a whole department called CAMP (Current Affairs Magazine Programmes) and programmes routinely known as DID (*Desert Island Discs*), RNR (*Radio Newsreel*), and FNIMN (*Friday Night is Music Night*). The corporation was full of bizarre-sounding personages whose job titles would soon, without the slightest sense of absurdity, be tripping off my tongue: 'Do you know whether ATOM (Assistant Technical Operations Manager) is in charge of moving the RNR stuff from SE13, or should I ask APOMXPOps?' (Assistant Programme Operations Manager External Programme Operations). It all made perfect sense after a while.

The careers handout was reasonably plain-spoken:

POAs are responsible for the artistic and technical operation for all studio programmes in Radio; artistic in that a POA, working for a Producer, must be able to interpret the effects which the latter wishes to achieve, and technical in that these effects can only be obtained by the knowledge and intelligent operation of the equipment. It involves a number of often complementary operations including the setting up of a studio for recording or transmission; effecting a proper sound balance; controlling and mixing on the studio panel; monitoring for programme quality; recording, editing and reproduction on tape of music and speech; playing all types of discs and selecting and often devising sound effects in studios or on tape or disc.

We must, it said, combine 'artistic flair with technical aptitude and possess a considerable degree of manual dexterity'. It also, rather threateningly, demanded 'previous elementary knowledge of electricity, magnetism, sound and acoustics, microphones and tape recorders' as well as tact, quick thinking, calm in emergencies and physical fitness. The description also made it clear that because it was an 'exacting' technical job, 'this work is not regarded as an automatic stepping stone to more senior posts in production or other departments in the BBC'.

Reading it now, I am struck by the essential unsuitability for the job of a clumsy, shy, scientific illiterate with an English degree. Yet I longed for it. At the interview, I was gently asked why on earth I was not applying for a news trainee post, learning to be a reporter or producer.

'Not interested,' I said grandly. 'I want to work the *gear*.' A few probing questions elicited the fact that apart from the stuff about teeny magnetic bits on the tape all changing positions when you recorded — wheee! — I had no technical knowledge, nor much commonsense. The board sighed, and the chairman said:

'You're overqualified. You'll get bored.'

'No, I won't,' I said.

'You will'.

'Won't.'

They gave in. After a few days, I got a stiff little letter telling me that I should take up my traineeship on Monday, 18 October, 1971 at a training salary of £1,137 per year, rising to £1,205 if I passed the course and achieved a post. It was all a bit like joining the Navy.

Secure in this exciting if incongruous future I bought the cheapest reel-to-reel tape recorder I could find, and spent the summer holiday practising recording myself and my brother hitch-hiking through West Cork, and laying down a number of rambling, dubiously authentic songs in the pubs. I found the tape a year ago, in a house move. Mice had nibbled it to oblivion.

4

Wow and Flutter

Today it is the Langham Hilton, but until the BBC woke up one morning and noticed the value of central London real-estate, the Art Deco building in question was haphazardly and wastefully devoted to the Corporation's purposes. It held a mixture of underused offices, some draughty and reputedly haunted overnight bedrooms for announcers, and most of the radio training facilities. The BBC Club sprawled across the ground floor in Palm Court splendour, and the shaky old 1930s lifts took you up to dusty classrooms and dummy studios where the tyro POA could learn the craft.

I arrived early, and slipped into the pillared church of All Souls, Langham Place so as not to be seen hanging around. In there I found a number of efficient-looking people setting up microphones for the 10.15 broadcast of the *Daily Service*, which was still done live. This provided a valuable training for outside broadcast engineers, since if they had any problems they had only to trot across the zebra crossing to be back at base. I watched them for a while as they plugged in leads and frowned over consoles, then wandered out again and spent some time staring up, respectfully, at the mighty ships' bows of Broadcasting House and Eric Gill's statue of

Prospero sending out Ariel. I already knew the story, from 1928, of how Gill made Ariel's penis too big and the BBC governors insisted on shortening it. I did not know the equally immortal remark that the sculptor made on completing his work for Reith and his romantic Roundheads: 'Comic, though,' said Gill scornfully, 'the BBC kidding itself that it may be likened to a prince putting the world to rights and its bally apparatus likened to a sort of heavenly spire.'

That's always been the trouble with the BBC. The moment you begin to wallow in a happy reverence for it, somebody — often from close to its heart — punctures the illusion. Yet in those days it was still possible to feel a real frisson of reverence for the Corporation. It had gravitas, it had painfully high standards. It had public respect (though sometimes more than it truly deserved) and it had a sense of mission. It was a benchmark, and it knew it.

Inside the Langham we were assembled in a classroom and impressed with our own smallness and the vast dignity of the organization we were joining. The training staff did not have any fancy modern ideas about 'empowering' us or respecting our youthful point of view.

'All graduates, are you?' said the one called Terry, grinning in a sinister manner behind a drooping black Zapata moustache. 'Right. Two things. We shan't be answering any questions starting with 'Why?' And if I ever catch any of you without your screwdriver and editing kit *at any time*, you're out.'

'Even in the pub, sir?' asked the most daring of us, Gordon House, who decades later seems to have become the Head of Radio Drama. He received a basilisk stare. We were introduced to the other trainers: Pete, a cheerful young man whose favourite response to our hideous mistakes was, 'Ooh-er, keep taking the tablets,' and Noel, who was classic Old BBC: grizzled, courtly and conventional to a fault, until you discovered that at the end of the day he hauled on full motorbike leathers over his suit and sped off home on a big Hell's Angel number with gleaming exhaust and a dodgy silencer.

Before the technical training we went through the ritual of Induction. This involved a bit of chat about welfare and pensions, and then a viewing of a rather dated COI-type film called *This Is The BBC*, which majored heavily on shots of Broadcasting House with rings of sound emanating visibly from it, and of well-dressed announcers saying 'BBC News' sternly into large black microphones. There was very little indeed about Radio 1, and a great deal about symphony orchestras, newsreaders, and foreign correspondents.

Once inducted, we began to be trained. I remained as entranced with the technicalities as ever, probably because after four arts A-levels and three years agonizing over Beowulf and Herbertson and Miltonic subtexts, it was liberating to learn scientific facts and studio protocols by heart, and to be debarred from ever asking the question 'why?' This was just as well: some of the machines we were trained on were

51

models which had actually gone out of service years before, but were kept on in the syllabus — 'like Latin' as Noel said — because it was considered morally bracing for us to learn them.

Take, for example, the business of starting a record. Today, it is generally a CD and is an instant matter: you push the button and the music starts. Even playing old vinyl records is almost instantaneous: only a year after I started, new generation turntables ran up to speed so fast that there was no need to do what we did in 1972. This was to find the start of the music (by wobbling the record to and fro against the needle, as with tape on a tape-head) and then wind back one-third of a revolution, so that the final business of starting the record involved three movements. Start turntable with right hand just a moment before the cue, let it run one-third of a revolution, and with other hand whip open the fader on the front of the machine, so that only clean sound ('modulation' we learnt to call it) emerges, and no crackle.

The training was made extra complicated because we were also expected to learn how to play obsolete 78 rpm records on a far older machine, the venerable and utterly obsolete TD7. The last few banks of these had been trundled over to the Langham in all their glossy black Bakelite glory to torment us. With these, you had to wind the record back *three and a half* revolutions to have any chance of its getting up to speed, make a chinagraph mark where the sound began, and count your yellow blob whizzing round three and a half times before whipping open the fader. The whole horror was compounded by the need to find the right place on the record with a wavy, wobbly Vernier scale not always very faithfully connected to the playing arm.

Not only music, but sound effects for plays and features came off grams. So if you were detailed off as grams player in a complex mini-programme exercise you would have to skip along a bank of machines, of different kinds, starting turntables, counting revolutions, whipping open big black faders and closing others, while an equally panicked colleague worked the mixing desk. So one of you smashed open wrong channels, uttered hysterical little shrieks, and tried to do elegant cross-fades while the other started turntables at the wrong speed, failed to open machine faders, dropped the needle on the wrong track and generally fouled up.

The 'manual dexterity' demanded in the job description proved a bit of a hurdle to many of us arts graduates. Mind you, there was not much percentage in being a science graduate either: the trainers made sure that nobody got too confident. ('Right. Today, we're gonna talk about stereo. Anybody here got a degree in Physics? Right, give me a hand moving this table . . . ') However, when it came to making up plays for our drama-studio exercise, we were right on the case. Gordon, the one who in the millennium year became Head of Radio Drama, claims that he still has a recording of me playing Piglet in his *Winnie-the-Pooh* condensation. At that point it was rather safer to have me playing Piglet than playing grams.

But gradually we became better at it. Whenever we did, the trainers sprung a new surprise on us: possibly the worst of them was a dummy exercise done as if live, when a few of us were made to use a studio setup even more obsolete than the rest of them, the dreaded OBA8. What nobody told us was that due to some hideous electronic quirk in its 1940s innards, every time you opened one channel — say, for a new tape or microphone — the level on all the others would drop, as if you had turned on an extra tap in a plumbing system. I think Gordon actually squealed at one stage, and I know that one highly strung girl (not me) had to be slapped out of hysterics when Big Ben suddenly came up unexpectedly, striking the quarter-hour during a supposedly clean Greenwich Time Signal.

It was a remarkably good grounding, though. These training studios were linked together, and linked to the time signal and the live microphone in Big Ben; for the 'White Network' near the end of the course, one of the instructors represented control room and the rest of us took over studios and contributed our live programmes, strung together, in the right order at fifteen-minute intervals as if it were real. We had to plug and cross-plug great baffling jackfields with cotton-covered leads, set up tape machines to thousand-cycle tone, play tapes and grams, flash codes to control room, do announcements, and manage four different kinds of studio desk, from the dinosaur OBA8 to the flashiest new Type D — a device so contemporary that it actually had fader knobs that pushed up and down (as on your hi-fi) rather than circular ones where you revolved a black disc over white space. We learned how to check the level of every piece of programming, constantly and instinctively, on the PPM or Peak Programme Meter, and were warned that for World Service we must peak it consistently higher to smash through short-wave noise and deliver Auntie's voice clearly to distant dominions of palm and pine.

We learned that the clock is everything, and must be checked before every transmission; and that there is no forgiveness for 'finger trouble', because if a tape is played in at double speed or half-speed (and some were 15 and some were 7½ inches per second, and woe betide anybody not double-checking) then it is a terrible, terrible disaster and Brings the Corporation Into Disrepute.

There was a lot of talk, back then, of Bringing The Corporation Into Disrepute. I suppose it was left over from Reith. You could do it by failing to pay your TV licence (a sacking offence), by muddling up the labels on transmission tapes, putting out an uncorrected retake, crashing sound into the pips, bungling a fade, or — worst of all — by forgetting to put the studio out of Rehearsal Mode and into Transmission Mode. The result of this was that you broadcast studio talkback to the nation. To this day nothing — absolutely nothing — makes a producer sweat like the thought that informal instructions to his presenter might be heard by the listener. 'Wind him up, he's boring' or 'Kill the Chancellor' are the least disastrous examples.

At the Langham in the 1970s there was little pity for human weakness. 'Amateur night, then, is it?' the trainers would snarl. To this day, hearing a technical mistake on the radio makes me shiver and sweat, whereas a presenter's gaffe or confusion only makes me smile at their humanity. 'Just get it bloody well right,' Terry would say, and sigh, and we would long to be infallible.

We listened, intently, to tape faults. We learned to hear the slightest drop-out or moment of dead space caused by a bad edit or a faulty reel; we were taught to wince at the slightest wow or flutter, to fear stretched or buckled tape, to filter out hiss and rumble, and never, ever to lay a recorded tape down on one of the vast, powerfully magnetic five-foot tall loudspeakers that hunched in the corner of studios like malevolent wardrobes. We did a spell of stereo training, at which I was spectacularly bad, and were warned against the risk of accidentally sitting in a node. We learned to identify induction, one-leggedness and howlround. We were briefly instructed in the art of 'spot effects', in which rather than struggle with some damned gramophone you got to make the noises for a drama yourself, with bits of coconut and fake doors and gravel pits to crunch your footsteps in. We learnt to track faults by thinking logically all down the line, eliminating suspects all the way from microphone to plug, to lead, to wall-plug, to jackfield, to channels on the desk. We learned to reply disdainfully to queries from distant control rooms with the immortal engineer's phrase, 'It's all right leaving me . . . '

And we edited with blades and chinagraphs, because a great part of the job of a POA was to edit tape under the direction of a producer (today, old union powers being broken and forgotten, they mainly do their own, with or without a computer). I was still rather good at editing tape, having a head start from Radio Oxford. I always loved it, and developed a delight in the way that natural speech — vox-pops in the street, or hesitant interviews — could be improved, speeded up, de-ummed, made clearer, and generally enhanced by the use of a razor blade. The pleasure of it was that when you tidied people up, they often ended up sounding more like their real selves than they had in the original.

I liked listening to speech and sentence patterns, over and over again, as you must do when you edit; that, I suppose, took me back to the skills picked up in three years of intense literary criticism. I knew and loved the way that voices sound. The fact that you ran the human voices fast, like squeaky chipmunks, then slowly like elephants roaring, only made the effect more delightful when at last you replayed the doctored speech properly, and it sounded like somebody speaking right next to you in the room. It was like being a surgeon, meddling with the very stuff of life, blood and breath and spit.

We were informed that to falsify the meaning

of an interview, or any speech on tape entrusted to us, would Bring the Corporation Into Disrepute; and that even if a producer ordered it we must query that order. Nonetheless, when we could sneak into editing channels for private practice, we followed the immemorial habit of radio technicians by cutting up old Royal Christmas Broadcasts into pleasing gibberish. ('On our tour of Kenya we met / Eskimos / bringing / my husband / Commonwealth / pudding.')

All this went on for two months. Then we were sent for two months each to Broadcasting House — where Radios 2 to 4 were made — and to Bush House on the Aldwych, the home of the overseas services funded by the Foreign Office but administered and edited by the BBC.

I went first to Broadcasting House, and liked it far less than I had expected. The studios were ludicrously overmanned by modern standards, and the trainee's job was often to 'trail', which meant standing like a fool, miserably watching someone a little bit senior starting a tape or a gram deck three or four times during a two-hour session. POAs were in the process of being renamed Studio Managers, with various re-arrangements of responsibilities between them and control room engineers; there was a curious tension which I was too new to understand, a secret war between a new set of rather uppity, artistic but technically less literate operators, and a cadre of ex-engineers with chips on their shoulder who knew damn' well how all the kit worked but were unsure of themselves when asked by an earnest Schools Radio producer to 'give it a sort of fuzzy dream-sequence feel, sort of Buñuel'.

On one such occasion a schools drama producer asked for a piece of music to be cut and resumed in a random pattern — sharply, poppingly, without fading — to express the way some light-bulbs don't work on the Albert Bridge. The senior POA insisted that this was not possible; you had to fade. The only alternative, she said, was to cut bits of blank tape into the recording, which would take ages; or to plug and unplug, which would cause a crackle. Unwisely, fresh from my training course, I pointed out that we could do the business instantly by just flicking a black rotary switch called the Tape Control Panel above the jackfield, thus routing the music away from the studio output. I was right, but the subsequent hatred directed at me by the main operator was not worth the triumph.

My only really happy moments in those training months at Broadcasting House were when I was sent to put up microphones for *Music and Movement* — thus gaining a satisfying sense of coming full circle from those sessions with the old valve radio at Walberswick village school — and the glorious days when I was sent to do spot effects (FX, in the land of initials). My favourite job was on a big, rather pointless detective play directed by one David Godfrey, who was extremely Old BBC with faint touches of Noël Coward at the edges. For three blissful days I crunched in the gravel pit, slammed the fake door, and ran to and from the Spot FX Store. This was a sort of Steptoe junkyard reached through an underground tunnel and manned by a dozily dedicated BBC Spot Librarian. He could instantly put his hands on pebble-drums to simulate marching, numerous grades of thunder-sheet, and forty different kinds of squeak ('this does a very good sash window, pre-war . . . that one's more of an Army officer's boot, you sort of grind the wheel against the leather flap . . . ').

David Godfrey told me, on the second day and with much mwah-mwah appreciation, that I 'did the best bedsprings he had ever heard'. I was thrilled, since I had invented the effect myself by combining a horsehair pad with some old car springs lashed to the blade of a canoe paddle. I adored being down in the big studio with the actors, living off my wits, darting around from microphone to microphone and being amiably joshed by the BBC rep cast (especially Olwen Griffiths, who specialized vocally in dogs, cats, and whimpering babies).

My finest moment came, though, when in a fit of creativity David called down the talkback: 'Libby darling — could we *hear* the Alsatian running downstairs? OK, darlings, go again — on the green — and pause to listen to the dog . . . ' I froze, looked at the wooden FX staircase in the corner, then ran to it and, bang on cue, clattered my fists and scrabbling fingernails down, in the manner of a dog skittering on its claws.

'Perfect!' sang out the producer, and I was

happy for the rest of the day.

Otherwise, it was a troubled two months. BBC perfectionism, as interpreted by radio middle-management, verged on neurosis. Part of the Corporation's sense of self resided in nothing ever going wrong, even the smallest thing. It was not, I think, a particularly creative time in radio. Television was storming ahead excitingly, luring the innovators and the louchely inventive. Too much of the radio service was resting on its old laurels and recycling its own old triumphs. Possibly this was why the tiniest technical infringement of standards brought on something close to hysteria.

I see myself, at that time, scuttling endlessly along those curved corridors with piles of tape from TIU (Tape Issue Unit, didn't you guess?) in my arms, anxiously looking for the next studio, terrified of being late or bringing the wrong kind of reel. Sometimes, even today, on certain floors of Broadcasting House I feel a rising juvenile panic, a sense that I should be elsewhere and am definitely in trouble. One day, a programme I had recorded (my sole duty all day being to fetch and put on a large reel of tape) turned out to contain several momentary drop-outs. It was not the kind of thing anybody at home, listening to any quality of radio, would be likely to notice. It was not a music tape, nor a stereo programme. Just some documentary, suffering from a couple of teeny glitches. It transpired that the cause was the tape I was issued by TIU — which was a reclaimed EMI brown one, not the virgin BASF newly prescribed for such uses. It was not my fault. Nonetheless I was called up by my worried little boss and given an impressive lecture on how such a thing must never, ever happen at the BBC again, and how ashamed I must be to be associated with it.

Which was irritating. On the other hand, in some ways the quiet technical perfectionism of the time was inspiring. One of the best jobs was to help Alan Athawes in a little room on the fifth floor called QCR (Quality Control Room). His job was to listen to faulty tapes, and if possible salvage valuable material, often for Sound Archives. We played all day with infinitely variable speed adjustments and with filters; top filters, rumble filters, notch filters to nip out one rogue frequency where the distortion lay. It refined my ear, as a musician's ear is refined by constant critical listening. After you had done this training, you might get posted for a day or two to the Gramophone Library or to Sound Archives and made to transfer old material on to fresh tapes, with similar improvements. I spent a lovely morning producing a cleaner version of an ancient 78 rpm ballad:

If those lips could only speak!
If those eyes could only see!
If those beautiful golden tress-es
Could be there in real-it-ee!
If I could only take your hand
As I did when you took my name!
But it's only a be-yoo-ti-ful picture
In a be-yoo-ti-ful golden frame!

See? I have not heard the song from that day to this, but I can sing every note. It was work which made you concentrate, passionately. There are — or were — many discs in the Sound Archives which I revelled in equally as I copied them off for some producer or other: interviews with silver-vowelled Edwardians caught just in time, wartime commentaries, J.B. Priestley, Bernard Shaw, the famously cross old man in Tunbridge Wells being interviewed by an upmarket young woman ('I don't know what you want me to say. You tell me and I'll say it'). And once, I spent six hours in a recording channel just making a copy of David Davis, late of *Children's Hour*, reading *The Wind in the Willows* with such plaintive emotion that all alone on my high operator's stool in the soundproof box, with only my tape machines and PPM for company, I wept real, happy, sentimental tears. To this day you have only to say 'Ohhh, Ratty!' in a soft David Davis voice to make me snivel.

I lived, during this time, in a rather depressing bedsit in a flat south of King's Cross with two girls much older than myself. Christmas came and went, and I found myself scheduled for duty early on New Year's Day. Rather than spend New Year's Eve sitting in a dusty bedsit two floors above an office equipment shop on the Gray's Inn Road, writing my blood group in my new diary, I timidly asked the punctilious little Scotsman who was in charge of us whether I might have permission from him to ask another permission from the Current Affairs department to watch some of the overnight transmission of the *Today* programme. They were experimenting that year with a live broadcast over the midnight hour, with Robert Robinson and John Timpson. Artfully, I made the case that it would be useful for me to observe high-speed news work in case I applied in the future to work in that area.

To my surprise all the various levels of authority agreed; and so I saw in New Year 1972 in the corner of the *Today* control room, squeezed alongside a gramdeck to keep out of the way of the important-looking producers with stopwatches round their necks, and the editors and reporters who strolled in and out with plastic cups full of whisky in their hands. I gazed raptly through the glass at two legendary figures, the authentic deep-voiced BBC men so powerful in their presence that they had had to be banned from the convent bathroom long ago. There was John Timpson cracking ho-ho jokes (at which I laughed extravagantly, while standing in his eye-line behind the glass — presenters love a visible audience to look happy). There was Robert Robinson uttering long, complicated, well-scripted witticisms while the studio lights bounced off his fine domed forehead.

Midnight struck, and we all smirked. It was a very BBC moment. I felt rather proud to be part of it, but had absolutely no presentiment that one day I would belong on their side of the glass. I still did not want to be a performer. I only wanted to play with the equipment, collect sounds and weave them into deep private impressions to pass on.

And, of course, to be praised for doing good bedsprings. I sometimes think the secret of happiness is not having much ambition. I walked home to Gray's Inn Road in the small hours, alone and quite content.

5

This is London

Bush House, home of the BBC World Service and its clutch of foreign-language services since 1940, stands between the Aldwych and the Strand and forms the widest slice of that great curved wedge. Built in 1910 as one of the world's grandest office buildings, it has never actually belonged to the BBC. Indeed, Auntie is due to be turfed out before the century is much older, in favour of some global bank or preening corporation (which will probably not put up with the present interior decor). Even today, it is a target for anti-globalization demonstrators every Mayday because the Inland Revenue has a department there.

Yet all over the world, for the generations that lived through the Second World War and the turbulent half-century after it, Bush House spells not oppression but liberty, and the BBC imprint will be on it forever. Its pillared dignity and labyrinthine interior could hardly be a better symbol of the Corporation in its noblest role. If the nautical, Art Deco, faintly camp, once-fashionable whimsy of Broadcasting House fittingly represents the domestic services, Bush House is more like an offshoot of wartime Whitehall: dour, massive, Churchillian. It is just the building from which to say in a resonant and authoritative tone, 'This — is — London'; just the building from which you would expect 'Imperial Echoes' and 'Lilliburlero' to crash out, announcing the news to captive nations. Bush House is a great grey serge nanny of a building with her petticoats laced with the red of speeding double-decker buses: just the girl you want on your side in a fight for liberty, to teach you English in a land where English is treason, to punch her way through Soviet jamming and Pacific storms.

If you are twenty-one, fairly broke, adrift in London for the first time with a very poor taste in men and a private life of hot and cold running humiliations, there is absolutely no better place to work. This is the case particularly if you are a studio manager (or POA, as we were still designated) because Bush is of its very nature a twenty-four-hour building. This means that your shifts, and your colleagues' shifts, run all round the clock; so when you are off duty, abandoned or tearful or a bit drunk in the West End, there is always this big solid stone Mummy to come back to. You have your ID pass, and it is as valid at 3 a.m. after a disastrous date as it is at 9 in the morning when you are actually working. If you belong to Bush you can go into the canteen or the POA common room, and whatever the hour you will find somebody you know and be sure of brief, soothing human contact and the loan of a tenner to get home.

On many nights I did this. I might be comforted by finding some fatherly World Service announcer with whom to flirt decorously at the coffee counter, or braced by meeting a couple of scornful night-shift colleagues ready to inform me that my lipstick had migrated up my face. If I was lucky, I would be offered advice by some kinder friend with headphones round her neck and an armful of tapes, who would find time to listen to the latest disaster in the fifteen minutes between *English by Radio* in C15 and *Hõla Paraguay!* in the South Wing basement. Moreover, the canteen food with which I consoled myself in the wee small hours was better in 1972 than the food on any other BBC premises. Real Spaniards, real Indians, real Poles would absolutely not have put up with the junk that passed for pizza, curry or dumplings in London at that time.

I fell in love with the place. Perhaps because I had had such a peripatetic childhood, it calmed and entranced me. Although professionally it was seen as rather a dead end, my two-month training attachment to Bush House ended with my opting — very enthusiastically — to stay there in my first permanent BBC studio manager post. Unkind colleagues pointed out that it was just as well that I liked it, since I had failed my stereo training module and would have been something of a pariah at Broadcasting House. But in any case Bush was wholly beguiling: the oddest job in the world, and not without challenge.

Here, trainees were not required to trail around respectfully after their betters. We were immediately treated as a resource by the hard-pressed duty director of operations, a gruff chap who lived in a cave lined with charts and rotas next to our common room. He greeted our new intake with a brusque: 'Right — good — now the main thing is punctuality. You will arrive *fifteen minutes* before the formal start of your shift, and you will not be late. I don't care if you've been in bed with the Director-General, you will *not be late.*'

Whereas in Broadcasting House in the seventies there were always POAs standing idle, and studio bookings for a simple fifteen-minute programme would stretch into interminable hours, everything at Bush was pared to the bone. Apart from the World Service — as complex as a twenty-four-hour Radio 4 — there were all the 'sections': Russian, Hungarian, Bulgarian and Serbo-Croat, Thai and Japanese, Spanish, Portuguese, Japanese, Hausa, Swahili, Arabic, Turkish . . . Today the BBC still broadcasts in forty-three languages; then, it may have been even more. None of us ever stopped to count.

We merely belted from one studio to the next, often at fifteen-minute intervals, to meet whichever preoccupied expatriate was scheduled to pump out news about Britain and the world. We would bring whatever was needed from our own stock cupboard: a disc of 'Imperial Echoes' for *Radio Newsreel*, or a rather pleasant, soupy version of the sea song 'Admiral Benbow', which for some reason always introduced the news in Japanese. Then we would sit down, glance at the schedule to see whether we had to put in a Greenwich Time Signal, Big Ben, or the blast of 'Lilliburlero' which was piped permanently all round the building, and make sure that the studio tape machines were working. Then we would wait for the anxious pattering of feet as the producer — or presenter, or hybrid of the two — came belting along the corridor and burst open the swing door.

Sometimes they were only going to read a news bulletin, so all the operator had to do was sit back and make sure that the meter kicked up to six. Sometimes it was more complex. Most of the non-live material, whether on tape or library discs, was brought along by the sections themselves, and had to be played by remote control from the desk (whereas at Broadcasting House there would have been a separate tape operator, maybe even a third hand to start the grams). You never knew quite what bag of tricks they would bring, and this contributed to the general excitement of the job. After the nervy perfectionism and essential dullness of much of the Broadcasting House work, there was a certain wild élan about Bush House production. Many temperaments, many exiles, many emotions were mewed up together behind its great pillars.

The first live transmission I ever put out — taking sole responsibility all the way from the preparation of the desk to the flashing signal to Control Room that we were ready to go live — was with some rather new Bengali producers who had got some kind of a scoop. They rolled in with three minutes to airtime and whammed down a script for me. The older man produced a reel from his flapping garment and said, 'This is the tape — cross-fade between band 1 and band 2.'

This is impossible: if you want a cross-fade, you have to put the tape on two different reels. I said so, and his face fell. It had been drummed into us that you never, ever imperil a whole transmission by doing last-minute work which should have been done elsewhere, but I could not resist it. He wanted his temple bells to fade quietly behind the interview, and he should have his dream. I would not let the customer down, not on my first solo job. I ripped the first band off the tape and stuck it hastily to a reel of yellow leader-tape somebody had left on the floor, set it up and got on the air just in time, adrenaline pumping, heart thudding. Afterwards, when he had said his goodbyes to the listening sub-continent, the dark young man bounded out of the studio and kissed my hand.

What more could a girl ask? The last programme I had assisted on, over at Broadcasting House, was a Radio 2 music magazine with a legendarily 'lovable' host. We were doing two Christmas programmes back-to-back, and as the first one concluded, the matinee idol with his deep voice intoned, 'Good night — and at this blessed season of Christmas, God bless you.' Then he stumped out into the cubicle and snapped at the senior POA on the desk, in a rather higher voice: 'Has that silly little bitch got the discs for the next programme ready?' Startled, I said from my corner, 'Huh, and God bless *you* too, mate,' and was later told off at great length about the importance of Not

Upsetting The Presenter. Today I could probably have sued the old boor.

But there was none of that at Bush, not ever. There were rows and tantrums, and occasionally a furiously pious White Russian would shriek at you for sacreligiously fading the Apostles' Creed (probably because she had mistimed it and you had a time signal to catch). But everyone forgave, and all the sections were delightful in their different ways. You had to watch yourself a bit with the Arabs in the night, and even more with the Latin-Americans, who had a long transmission in the small hours and liked to while away their time, between jabbering sports news and introducing José Feliciano records, by making passes at the younger female operators. It was not a wise shift on which to wear your more transparent 1970s cheesecloth gear, even in the heat of summer.

The Latino faction were forgiven everything, though, for their *joie de vivre*. One night, when there was not much to do because they were reading all the commentaries live, the POA at the desk was getting on with a patchwork quilt. The boss swayed up to her, leaned flirtatiously over her shoulder and said, 'Ah, your work is like you, so beautiful — do you need more cloths?'

'Yes,' she said, whereon he tiptoed into the studio where his colleagues were reading at high speed — live to a whole continent — and cut off each of their ties just under the knot. He brought them back as tribute to the patchworker. The other Latins read on, dark eyebrows twitching. One is, after all, a professional.

Clearly, most of the transmissions themselves were gobbledegook to me. That only added to the romance of this immense radio experience: when I edited tape in polysyllabic staccato Turkish, or carefully played discs of the Koran end-to-end, trying to make the pause between verses natural and harmonious with the pace of the chanting, or spooled through a tape of clicking Hausa, I was connected back to those childhood nights under the bedclothes tuning into France and Holland and Albania and the rhythm of the beating world.

With such a remorseless workload, even the duffers among us grew better and better at the manual tasks, and after years of academe the achievement of technical mastery brings a particular joy. I rejoiced in the sheer exhilaration of whipping open the GTS fader just in time, or keying in grams and tapes dextrously by remote control if my tape operator hadn't turned up. I loved to play our version of Russian Roulette with the Big Ben fader, too: the legendary clock has a microphone in its tower, constantly live to a dedicated fader on every main Bush desk. During a dullish transmission you could fade it up high to hear the distant roar of London traffic beneath the tower — then whip it out again just seconds before it struck, and listen on headphones to see how close you had been to disaster.

I even — after initial tremblings — grew to enjoy the minute amount of 'voice work' asked of Bush operators, announcing *English by Radio* programmes. 'BBC World Service. *English by*

Radio,' I said poshly, then whipped the microphone shut, terrified at my own daring, and pulled down the little plastic-coated switch to start the tape.

The predominance of foreign-language broadcasts also meant that if you did have the treat of an English-language job on your rota, you looked forward to it all day. *Radio Newsreel, Outlook*, or the letters programme were great events. Sometimes there was even a play: I got to do spot effects for a World Service production of *The Second Mrs Tanqueray*, and tear up a letter melodramatically, 'into small pieces' according to the script, while the late Dorothy Tutin (a hell of a good catch for World Service Drama) did the heavy breathing on the other side of the microphone. Actually, to tell the truth we floor staff got a bit fed up with Dorothy Tutin, because there was a scene with some pears she had to bite into, and we rather hoped to nab the spare ones. But she bit a different pear on every take, so there weren't any fresh ones left. Prima donna.

Altogether it was the most surreal yet cosy first job anybody could ask for. A strange life, though: I do not know anywhere else that runs a weirder shift system than Bush House did in those days. Nobody could opt for permanent days or permanent nights: you had to migrate round an eight-day clock system. Your first day had a 1500 start, your second a couple of hours earlier, and so forth, until just as your body was acclimatized to early waking, you hit a night shift — ending at 6 a.m. — and then had three days off. So there were no weekends, no regular evenings off to meet friends. The only constant people in your life were the rest of the dozen who worked on the same pattern as you, your 'clump', and that became almost a tribe. Clumps were, indeed, structured deliberately as such: every one seemed to have an older man and woman who were senior and reassuring, then a middling group of settled grown-ups, and then us babies stumbling along at the end under their watchful eye. So powerful is the clump-bond that although I was only at Bush for one year, thirty years ago, whenever I run into a fellow-clumper in some BBC studio now we greet one another like long-lost siblings. 'Muffin!' 'Hell-ooooh!'

After a period of this odd dislocated life, sleeping to no recognizable pattern, you got a fortnight of 'float shifts', filling the gaps in the schedule. A float could be anything except a full night, so for your social life it was even worse: nothing could be planned, no theatre ticket booked, no outing arranged in that fortnight lest you hit a row of four-to-midnights and lose all your evenings.

Shiftwork pleased me, though. It was an atavistic joy to be working with my hands, in the depths of the night when the nation was asleep. It felt like a privilege to carry my screwdriver for lining up Philips tape machines, my razor blades and tape for editing: suddenly I was part of a gruff Nevil Shute world of pit-stops and wartime aero mechanics, my tiny technical contribution vital to the safety of the droning bombers of BBC news as they winged across the globe. Well, as I have said, I maybe spent too much of my youth watching old films on telly. But truly, in the common room at Bush House during a 'flu epidemic or other staffing emergency, the atmosphere was often such that our boss, the DOA, might as well have had a squadron-leader's moustache, a labrador and a tin leg.

Shiftwork gave me a kinship with seedier workers too. If I happened to wear a short skirt or tight sweater I would find that in the morning, going home on the number 11 bus to new digs in Pimlico, I got conspiratorial winks of sympathy from the other working girls of the West End, as they yawned and pulled fake-fur coats over their skimpy night-time allure. 'Hard night, love?' There was a satisfaction in that, too. I had lived much abroad or at boarding-school in child-hood. To be accepted as belonging anywhere was an honour.

The odd hours took their toll. At two o'clock one morning, preparing to put out a Far Eastern tape alone in a basement studio, I heard the door open behind me, and someone came in and put a hand on my shoulder. I assumed it was the DOA, come to change my schedule for the night, so I glanced at the meter to check all was well, stretched, and turned to say hello. There was nobody there. The door was shut and motion-less; the hand was still on my shoulder. The South Wing ghost, no doubt. It felt very cold, and I was glad that my next job was up among the rorty Latinos on the fifth floor.

On other nights, after a day made sleepless by uncaring flatmates and car-door-slammers in the street, I would learn the meaning of the old nurses' expression, 'Three o'clock in the morning courage'. There are hours before dawn when your whole body yearns so desperately for the horizontal that you will snatch even three or four minutes on the common-room sofa. Begging a colleague to wake you, you sink on to grimy leatherette cushions with a moan almost of lust, and rise from it in utter despair. Yet I found at Bush, as I have often found again during years of shiftwork and on ocean passages in small boats, that fatigue and physical despair sharpen the senses. Being worn out, disoriented, and mildly confused as to what time of day it was could actually create an occasional explosive high. I danced down silent corridors sometimes with my armful of signature tunes; I did a silent jive to 'Imperial Echoes' behind the loudspeaker, where the announcer could not see me. On the rare transmissions where two operators were involved, and conversation a possibility, I greeted my clump-colleague with something extravagantly like love.

Alone, other moments shone. One night I had to announce an *English by Radio* tape in which the producers had devoted fifteen minutes to a word-by-word analysis of Don McLean's 'American Pie'. This hip, yet weirdly pointless, exercise drew my misty smallhours' attention to a fine point of concentration. As the recorded presenter explained the significance of the Chevy and the levée and the good ol' boys drinking whisky and rye, it seemed to me that I was being made party to the deepest secrets of the universe. I copied the tape and carried it around secretly for days, listening at every opportunity. I may have been a little mad.

Another time, a colleague had brought in a few old 78 rpm records to dub in the dull gaps of his watch. I had a mild crush on the lad, though only when he wore his yellow sweater, and joined him in an empty studio: together we listened to an early recording of Paul Robeson singing 'Ol' Man River' and he said softly: 'It was closer then, the time of slavery. You feel it.' *I git weary, and sick of trying, I'm tired of living and feared of dying* . . . The crackle and hiss of antiquity were part of the magic. We played it again, then went our separate ways, quite silent.

It was an eventful year: the year of Bloody Sunday, of aggravated bombing in Vietnam and then American withdrawal, of Idi Amin's expulsion of the Asians, the Nixon-Brezhnev pact, and so forth. I was less aware of it all than I might have been. World Service News is a ponderous and serious beast, and the dispatches of *Radio Newsreel* in those days still punched at a Reithian weight. Nothing made me understand the significance of what we were doing as keenly as the night when a university friend turned up in London after a spell of strenuous VSO in Burundi. She had been caught up in a territory affected by the tribal uprising, and stranded for a spell. She was quiet, awed at being inside the building which had spoken to her across half a world during the time of greatest fear. 'You can't know what that news meant to us,' she said quietly. I began to point out announcers she

78

would have heard — 'Over there's John Marsh, and that's Gerry Foster Norris — come on, let's say hello, they'll love to meet a satisfied customer.'

She pulled me back down into my chair. 'No — no, I couldn't. Let me just look.' She did not want the spell broken, or daylight let in upon the majesty of BBC World News. We drank our coffee and just gazed. And I spared her the classic disgraceful newsreader stories: of the time the cleaning lady roared into a live news studio with her Hoover blaring, or the other time that one newsreader came on duty drunk (well, he quite often did, but on this occasion he had crossed an invisible line). Majestically he began: 'In Paris today, Monsieur Pompidou . . . ' Then after an awful pause said, 'Mmm. Pompi-dou. 'S'a nice word. Shay it again. Pompi-pompi-pompidou . . . ' Then continued, word perfect, to the end.

A more focused interest stirred in me when I was sent to the Newsroom. This job involved no live studios, but permanent attendance in a cubicle — or 'channel' — with an editing machine and speaker, and another machine whose function was to record incoming dispatches. You harvested dispatches from correspondents covering Israel or Bangladesh or Vietnam or Nixon's visit to China. When each one called up, you threw the switch to record him (or, rarely, her), monitored the material on headphones, noted any fluffs or retakes, then cut them out, tidied it up with a top-and-tail, logged it and passed it to the editor of the bulletin,

Radio Newsreel, or the softer, more thoughtful *From our Own Correspondent* (FOOC, in BBC language. I lose count of the flippant exchanges over the teleprinter along the lines of 'Bill, thank you for the lovely FOOC', 'Don't mention it, darling, I enjoyed it too', etc).

It was pleasant in the Newsroom. I liked the combination of pressure and routine, surprise and long dull half-hours watching the television and yarning with the newsmen — mainly mature ex-Fleet-Street types with baggy grey cardigans and a polystyrene Cup-a-Soup rippling on their desks while they banged iron typewriters with two fingers. Gradually I began to take notice of the world news, and to knit my brow more thoughtfully than I ever had in the glorious days of student demonstrations in Grosvenor Square when black-and-white always made red. I was dimly aware, through the usual preoccupation with my own troubles, that it was a privilege to be processing news from the world and throwing it out again to that world as part of an organization still deeply respected everywhere. I was also, as a technician in sounds and voices, powerfully aware of the varying techniques and impacts of correspondents. Some were natural-born bores, others you always wanted to listen to, however crackly the line.

My finest hour came during the early-autumn, when the Olympics were on television. Olga Korbut, first of the flirty girl gymnasts, was mesmerizing the wholly male newsroom staff, and day after day I would work away in my recording channel unsupervised while they sat, grey cardigans stretched over majestic guts, Cup-a-Soups undrunk at their side, murmuring, 'Phewww . . . those girls must have such powerful . . . *thighs* to do that . . . ' One day, I had edited a whole *Radio Newsreel* by myself and written a running order before I could tear the duty lecher away from the latest set of enticing Mittel-European buttocks gyrating on the parallel bars.

I left Bush long before I was tired of it. I had spent a year there, and while I was a little weary of living in London I was not entirely happy at the thought of losing the dreamlike eight-day pattern, the fevered night-shifts, the kind little Indians and morose Russians and the polyglot babble of the canteen. But I was being thrown out of my flat anyway, a similar grade job had come up at Radio Oxford, and I suddenly longed to be somewhere smaller and greener, and where I could understand a bit more of the programmes I was putting out.

At the selection board interview the kindly, donnish station manager twinkled at me, making it fairly clear that after having done *Tourist Trap* and the university programme for them I was in with a good chance. The BBC personnel delegate, however, went through all the artful questions set down in the training-manual.

'What do you dislike about your present job?' she said heavily.

'Nothing. I love Bush House. It's magic.'

'There must be something you dislike?'

'Well . . . Arabic music. Drives me mad.'

81

'No, something in your *duties* that you dislike?'

'Playing Arabic music. Especially in the night. Creepy.'

'What do you hope for in the Radio Oxford post you have applied for?'

'That there won't be so much Arabic music.'

The station manager giggled behind his hand, Miss Personnel glared, but I got the job. I would be a station assistant, the most junior of four. I rented a truly terrible bedsitter with condensation running down the walls, and turned my back on London.

6

Community

BBC local radio changed the face of British broadcasting: there is no question about that. For all the scoffing of the networks, for all their uncool and chirpily provincial Alan Partridge image, the fact is that even those who never listen to them owe a great debt of gratitude to the local stations, because they breathed new life into the medium of speech radio. It was not before time.

These stations were always small, with barely twenty on the payroll including engineers. They have always been run on a shoestring and dependent on the enthusiasm of staff who work long hours without claiming, and on unpaid volunteers. From the first, because they ran on goodwill rather than the Civil Service rules of the main BBC, they revived something of the original wonder and fun which had fuelled the 1920s radio experiments. Their shoestring existence meant that even the humblest member of staff could rack up a wide and heady range of experiences, as if in a *Boys' Own* or star-is-born fantasy: ('There's nobody in the newsroom — the town hall's on fire — traffic backed up for a mile — quick, who's got a bike?' — and off speeds the ambitious reporter, tape machine in the bike basket.)

It also enabled strange, determined figures from the local communities to come forward and become small legends: like the country-and-western DJ on Radio Humberside who used to come over from Scunthorpe on the Humber ferry wearing his stetson, cowboy boots, chaps and leather-tasselled jerkin. He would present his programme in a cod American accent, but was in fact a crane-driver at the steelworks. He is also remembered as unique among broadcasters in that he had no teeth.

Another advantage of early local radio was that the audiences were relatively tiny, and miles away from the cautious, slow-beating corporate heart of the BBC in London. There was a 'directorate' in charge of local radio, but it was relatively benevolent and too preoccupied to interfere much in any one station (only stepping in to intervene when the manager succumbed to religious mania, drink, or the more florid sort of delusions about his role). Their remoteness from the capital kept most stations safe from the smart, whiny metropolitan newspaper critics, of whom the BBC's higher management tradition-ally lives in dread. So the new little stations could take risks, both editorial and technical. The prissy technical perfectionism of Broadcast-ing House could not touch them: as for news and features, the depth and range of a station's challenge to local councillors and troublemakers was left entirely up to the nerve of individual news editors.

Yet for all this they were still BBC, still free from advertising, still able to live on the legacy of trust and respectability from their distant parent. This sharing of the old Reithian mission added another ingredient to the mix: the beam of light, however refracted, still struck off the great domed forehead, and the simple conviction of being there 'to do good' in the community prevented the early stations from lurching downmarket into pap and pop.

Sometimes, of course, they simply failed. One of the first experimental stations was Durham, which had so few listeners that it got closed down and fused with neighbouring Radio Newcastle. My husband, as a young station assistant there, remembers that his first task of the day was to go through the phone book and invent record requests. Still, Radio Durham launched Kate Adie, which must be to its credit.

By and large, though, the experiment was a happy success and an immense enrichment to the range of UK radio. It was a pity when its expansion was frozen, in 1971, by the Heath government's decision that it would be more profitable to license sixty local commercial stations. Still, today thirty-seven BBC stations remain, and mop up a quarter of all radio audiences in the UK, second only to the pop Radio 1.

Equally importantly, from Newcastle to Cornwall a myriad different voices have come on to the air because of local radio. People have spoken who never would have been invited by the networks; unless perhaps as comical rustics or amusing locals in some patronizing show like the old *Down Your Way*. And — because BBC stations had pledged not to be primarily pop vehicles — the new voices were not all DJs but contributors to the more considered, communicative medium of speech radio.

It was a relaxed world, in spite of the hard work and long hours. Because being on Radio Bogtown was not a very big deal, and not likely to provoke critical editorials in the *Daily Telegraph*, producers were able to find maverick talent and personality in the local community and nurse it slowly. Pam Ayres was a secretary in Witney who sent in a poem about a battery hen to the Radio Oxford producer Andy Wright: he nurtured and encouraged her, slowly and carefully, until she evolved into a kind of national legend, of the type only thrown up today by the occasional TV docu-soap. At the other end of the scale, generations of university dons and scientists cut their broadcasting teeth on local radio interviews explaining their work (goodness, how shy they were at first!), and nerved themselves up after a year or so to face *Start the Week* or *Any Questions*. Because there were a lot of hours to fill and not many people, the local stations were from the start able to put voices and temperaments on the air which would never have made it through the neurotically fine sieve that was BBC network radio.

And frankly, because the BBC itself was a bit embarrassed and equivocal about local radio, London kept off its back. Not to put too fine a point on it, it was a place where you could have your disasters in private and learn all the faster for it.

The classic, self-deprecating local radio anecdotes reflect that time. 'Have you heard about the local station that had a phone-in on apathy, and nobody rang?' Not a joke. At Radio Oxford we once had a health phone-in on headlice, and nobody rang until after the fourth record. Despite fifteen minutes of increasingly desperate conversations between the presenter and an embarrassed community nurse, when the call came it went something like this:

PUNTER: Headlice! They're disgusting, I think it's terrible — '

PRESENTER: 'No, no, there's no shame in having headlice, they like clean hair, as we were just saying — '

PUNTER: 'Well, I think it's disgusting. I ride a moped, and the lorries and that, they never bloody dip their headlights for me — '

It could get surreal sometimes. But all the time, through the greatest absurdities and most ludicrous provincialisms, we were genuinely breaking new ground. This went down to the smallest technical details. While the networks were still lumbering around with overmanned and anxiously formal Outside Broadcast Units, we were dangling microphones out of the window on 30-foot leads hastily taped together because the Scout Band was too big to fit in the studio and had to play in the car park. While Radio 4 was experimenting with its first phone-ins, which were heavily screened productions with some schoolmarmish presenter ever ready to cut off dodgy callers before they could say a dreadful word like 'bum', local radio stations were way ahead. They just put every caller on the air without a tape-delay, and let them have their heads, lambasting local councillors in the studio or ranting on perilously about the latest stoppage at British Leyland.

We had the first radio cars: ordinary saloons with telescopic 26-foot UHF aerials on the roof, one per station, which were on the road every day, often from three or four successive locations. Three years later, when I went to *Today*, network news was just starting to deploy this technology with much sucking-in of teeth and shaking of heads at its riskiness. In my early days as a *Today* presenter we once had a fire-eater on (God knows why, but apparently it was topical) and a reporter was supposed to record him and run upstairs with the tape to put it on the air minutes later. I said, 'Let's do him live from the car park, much more buzz.' My fellow-presenter looked at me as if I was insane. Within the year, such a manoeuvre did not raise an eyebrow. By 1980 there was nothing unusual in a cabinet minister darting out of his house in his dressing-gown to be interviewed in a radio car parked outside by the breakfast programme. It was local radio which started all that.

Local stations adopted, as their manner, a curious hybrid of the three most popular networks — Radios 4 and 2, with an occasional hour or so of Radio 1. When we went off the air in the evening, we switched to rebroadcasting Radio 2, this being thought of as the station least likely to cause our listeners to retune. Radio Oxford, however, was actually rather closer to Radio 4 in its tone, with an almost suicidal willingness to schedule dense, carefully produced speech features, interviews and news magazines rather than the softer, chattier options which are popular now. It would have been cheaper and more relaxing to do what is now common: a whole morning's rolling programme with only two actual interviews, spun out and padded with traffic-news inserts, phone quizzes, matey banter between presenters, and a lot of easy-listening music. Instead of this, the early Radio Oxford opted to punch above its weight and schedule the day like a miniature Radio 4.

So there would be half-hour 'down your way' programmes with titles like *Hello, Steeple Aston*, documentaries into which intense work had gone for weeks, all-speech news magazines, and specialist programmes on gardening, nature, local history, and disability which were not merely 'inserts' in woffly magazines but properly built programmes with their own signature tunes and identities.

There was a lot of thought given also to uniting the two communities of Oxford city itself, town and gown, and some wonderful solutions emerged. Perhaps the best was Andy Wright's weekly session with Dr Bill Hassall, a charming elderly historian, in which listeners from the outlying industrial estates would write in asking for the history of their surname, and be met with erudite donnish enthusiasm and nuggets of arcane history: a simple, delightful

89

present from the university to the town. ('Ah, now Hughes *could* take us to the Huguenot immigration . . . ') All this programming was dense and laborious, and went beyond the station's original simple brief; it was in some ways a rash strategy, which led to a lot of fatigue. But it produced some valiant work and was done with considerable pride.

And if they had not done it, the listening would have been dire indeed. The modern agreements with music unions had not been signed, so the current option of padding everything with pop was not actually available. Under the 'Needletime' agreement with the musicians' unions we were very limited indeed in how much commercial music we could afford to play. One of the duty station assistant's jobs was to log every single piece of music with its duration, composer, performer and record company code, on hateful carbon forms. The three most important letters to us were NNT: non-needletime music. It still had to be logged, but did not need to be paid for and could be used without limit.

NNT fell into several categories. There was film soundtrack music (how grateful we were to *A Clockwork Orange* and *West Side Story*). There was 'illustrative' use (like playing the 'Pushbike Song' in an item on cycling). There was 'review' use, if you were introducing a new record. Then there were recordings by BBC orchestras, all paid up and presented in utility green paper sleeves (Strauss waltzes were the most palatable). And finally there were long, grim shelves full of music which had already been paid for by the BBC under some diabolical agreement, and titled CANADIAN TALENT LIBRARY.

Apart from a few Newfoundland folk songs delivered on decent whistles and accordions it was mainly evilly syrupy lift-muzak, going under titles like 'Toot Toot Gallop' or 'Swing Happy Swing'. You know the sort of thing: hotel-lobby background music with neither classical dignity nor rock rhythm to commend it. To this day, if I saw the white cover of a CTL disc I think I would burst into tears.

One of the dullest on-air jobs that the station had to offer for the first few months I worked there was a session called *Music till Midday* or *Mid-Morning Melody* (nobody could ever remember which it was, or cared much). Its function was to fill the gap between the eleven o'clock News and the noon programme, and there was no budget and no particular aim to it. Producers refused to have anything to do with this dead hour, so the duty station assistant — whose main job was menial announcing, tape playing, editing and logging — had to go into the studio with an armful of NNT records and somehow use up the time.

I was thrown into this in my second week. Mari, the senior SA, stuck her head round the door of the gram library where I was dutifully tidying up, and said, 'Hoy, I've got to go downtown and record something, so you'd better do *Mid-Morning Misery*. You know what to do? Good.' She vanished. It was to be the first time I ever went on the air live to say anything beyond a prim, repressive: 'This is London. And now, *English by Radio*', or such simple Radio Oxford announcements as, 'Gordon Kitchen with the News. Now it's six-thirty and time for John Simpson to say, *Hello, Witney!*'

Nobody seemed to think there was anything momentous about this rite of passage, with its heady editorial independence. Actually, nobody was available to worry. The producers were all off recording things, the news editor was staring glumly at the County Council agenda, and the other station assistant on duty was keeping well clear in case he had to do what he called *Music till Doomsday*. Swallowing hard, I scooped up some records and timidly crept into the main studio.

I wish I could say that when I emerged nearly an hour later it was to plaudits and cries of, 'Hey, kid, you did great! You'll be a star!' In fact, I doubt very much that anyone heard it at all. So perhaps it did not matter that I muddled up two record covers and announced a BBC orchestra pop styling of 'Yesterday' as a CTL performance of 'Chirpy Chirpy Cheep Cheep' by Swinging Sid Cheese and the Ontario Cheesettes.

And perhaps it did not matter either that my voice was a touch shrill with nerves and youth. I had by this stage been warned, by the rather aloof programme organizer, that while I could be tolerated as an announcer and possibly an interviewer, I should never think of myself, long-term, as being a broadcaster. 'Radio,' he said, 'needs contraltos. Think of Patricia Hughes.

Listeners just don't like high women's voices. Sorry, but there it is.' He stroked his beard a lot while delivering this verdict.

Actually, he was given further ammunition for this theory when, after the first time I was allowed to read the unimportant evening bulletin, no fewer than three listeners rang in to ask, 'Why is that little boy reading the news?' Still, being identified as a little boy got me clear of the more usual problem that women had on the radio in a nation whose media were still run by misogynistic public-schoolboys. An eminent woman announcer of the eighties told me once that whatever you did, however neutral and pleasant you sounded, a female voice would always be categorized instantly as one of the following: mumsy, tarty, Sloaney, dumb blonde or nagging schoolmarm. And she was right. They still are. Listen to any comedy show.

Mid-Morning Melody was also the only time when Brenda McNicholas, the longsuffering cleaner, could get into the main studio. So you would sit between your gramdecks, usually finishing off some logging from the morning programme, and try to give her nice long pieces of music to work in. At the end of each track you opened the microphone, back-announced the piece of music very slowly to fill time, then announced the next track in the hope that you had remembered to put it on the turntable (I had a recurring anxiety dream, in those days, that I would turn round and find a fruit pie rotating on the gramdeck instead of a disc, and that the needle would grate through the pastry

93

with a horrible shashing sound.) It was a courtesy, when you had started a new track and closed the microphone, to say to Brenda: 'Two minutes twenty-five seconds — dusting only, I think' or 'Seven minutes thirty, so it's a Hoovering record'.

Strauss' 'Blue Danube' was a particularly good Hoovering track; nearly nine minutes. The only problem was that Mrs McNicholas, like the rest of us, grew blasé after a while and failed to turn off her machine early enough. So a whole generation of impressionable Oxfordshire toddlers, mooching round the house with their mothers, must have grown up thinking that the proper ending of a Strauss waltz was '*Bom, bom, bom bom-bom da daaaaaaaa — oooowheeeeee-arrrrrrr,*' with the last stately notes of the orchestra shading prettily into the dying fall of a vacuum-cleaner. Possibly the worst track to do this with was Tchaikovsky's 'Waltz of the Flowers' from the Nutcracker Suite, whose last notes blend particularly eerily with a Hoover. Try it yourself sometime.

This cruel restriction on music gave particular cachet and importance to the disc jockeys, who got the lion's share of the needletime we actually were allowed. There was a GI from the American base at Upper Heyford who called himself Peanutz and raved in a suitably transatlantic way at weekends. That was not unlike Radio 1, though all his records had to be new and fall under the 'review' category of NNT. There was a daily drivetime request show called *Home Choice*, presided over in more stately fashion by kind, pretty Sally Bourdillon, rather after the school of *Forces' Favourites* on Radio 2. She had the right temperament for it, being a deeply, unfeignedly nice person. When Sally wished you a 'Happy Diamond Wedding' you knew that she meant it. Then there was a classical music programme which could have passed in a dim light for Radio 3, presented by a suave elderly chap in ginger suede shoes; a country music hoedown, and a jazz show done late at night in a hip, incomprehensible mutter by a nervous young man with black hair curling over his collar.

But possibly the most unlikely disc jockey of them all was Humphrey Carpenter, son of the former Bishop of Oxford, later to become the acclaimed biographer of Ezra Pound, Benjamin Britten, Denis Potter and Archbishop Runcie. This wild-haired, beaky figure of delirium was one of the founder-producers of Radio Oxford, and eventually married a calm, beautiful Welsh station assistant called Mari Prichard. He mostly did the morning programme, handling major interviews with crackling intelligence and aplomb; but on a Saturday morning he reinvented himself as DJ Humf, rather wilder than Kenny Everett, with a taste in mad stings, silly jokes, goonish sketches and quickfire gabbling patter which would still be highly marketable today on the most commerical of stations, were it conceivable that such a distinguished literary figure would take it up again. Humf and Mari walked around in matching *blue de travail* overalls from their

French holiday, and rowed off for weeks on a doughty expedition to find the source of the Thames with a tape recorder. Our more middle-Englandish colleagues found them 'odd' or affected; I thought they were intensely glamorous.

There were also various other satellite freelances, the most notable of whom was the children's entertainer Johnnie Chuckles, who was a local Punch-and-Judy man, complete with the usual ghastly throat-valve device called a 'swozzle' which makes Punch's voice. He had an imaginary creature called Froggie Mush who talked in this odd voice, and would hurl the swozzle in and out of his throat while interrogating Froggie on his live programme. Once, he swallowed it and had to let nature take its course for a day or two. It must have been the oddest entertainment on offer anywhere in the UK radio network: a radio Punch-and-Judy man with a manic imaginary frog.

Anyway, we were no Durham: with this formula Oxford built, over its first five years, an audience of over 100,000. Peanuts (or Peanutz) in national terms, but not at all bad.

* * *

Looking back now, I understand how this curious station came to straddle the different radio cultures of the day. The manager, Donald Norbrook, was very Old BBC indeed: almost Imperial BBC. You could have carved him on a Roman coin. A tall, balding, donnish figure with a sweet and slightly crazy smile, he had served in far-flung corners of the Commonwealth and come back, like Mike Henderson, to be a safe pair of hands in the last years before he retired. One of his favourite expressions was happily reminiscent of my bygone training course: 'Hmm, hmm, yes, good, I don't think that brought the Corporation into disrepute.'

At Christmas, like a proper patriarch, he held a party at his house with mince pies and mulled wine and all the staff singing carols round the piano. Looking around the ring of faces that first Christmas, relieved to be out of London despite the dank horror of my North Oxford bedsit, I tried to get the measure of them. Already in the station's short life, there were couples: Andy Wright, the best producer, and Sally, the *Home Choice* record presenter, later his wife; Nigel and Judith, both station assistants; Humphrey and Mari, spiky intellectuals.

There was Thomas Prag — in the 1990s to become a multiple Sony Award winner with his own Inverness commercial radio station — who was a morning presenter and producer, sharing the shift with Humf. There was Tony Adamson, now a national tennis correspondent but then more focused on the dreary business of covering Oxford United and local leagues. He did the country-and-western show, playing yowly tracks like 'Blanket on the Ground'. There was a proper Oxfordshire countryman, John Simpson, who was in charge of rural and farming matters; Mike Dickin, who had a boyish passion for cars, a broad red beard and a roving eye; and Sharon, who was the management secretary but far too clever for the job, and accordingly given to telling Donald's more importunate staff visitors where to go, in a bracingly stroppy tone. There were the engineers, Cliff and Derek.

In the Newsroom lived Gordon Kitchen, the ageing editor, exuding gravitas, Bill Rennells, his deputy, full of fey mischief and picaresque memories of life on the *Dover Argus*, and Colin Fenton, the local news-agency man, who worked on contract with the Newsroom and brought us the authentic, opportunist feral reek of Old Fleet Street. When Colin limped past and fixed you with his squinting eye, beneath his fading floppy ginger hair, you were wise to clam up. He valued his 'lineage' in the *News of the World*, did Colin.

They were all pretty nice to me. I had, after all, hung around there as a student, and knew my place. I was also unattached and childless, and therefore came in useful not only for working overtime, weekends and bank holidays without complaint or extra pay, but as a babysitter to an exuberantly fertile set of colleagues. In fact, it was one of those workplaces you only find once or twice in a lifetime: just the right size, just the right mix of ages. It became a large extended family with all the necessary *Cold Comfort Farm* accessories of eccentrics, obsessives, walking sexual disgraces, secret drinkers, feuding rivals, brooding jealousies, rows, treacheries, flirtations, and blessed family jokes which make it all worthwhile.

Just to illustrate the last four, let me recall one row — a couple of years later, when Donald

Norbrook had left — in which Tony Adamson stormed into the new manager's office to complain about me, and was assured that he would be backed. Twenty minutes later I stormed into the manager's office to complain about him, and was told the same. This, apparently, was a new management technique called 'Open Door', which the boss had learnt in a BBC think-tank the previous weekend. By lunchtime Tony and I had cleared the air with a bit of shouting and arm-waving and a hug, and on comparing notes we discovered that we had both been promised conflicting resolutions of the problem. So we stormed back through the open door together and confronted the cowering manager, told him our solution, and went out to the pub to celebrate.

It was also that brief golden period, between the liberating, cheeky 1960s and the rise of politically correct paranoia in the 1980s, when it was still possible to sit on a colleague's knee or indulge in playful wrestling matches without finding yourself in front of an industrial tribunal. All in all, Radio Oxford in the early 1970s was an excellent place to work. On the twenty-first anniversary of its foundation, in 1991, without the slightest encouragement from the current regime, a group of producers from this period organized a reunion party for everyone who remembered the first manager, Donald.

It was a most wonderful and riotous party, with all but one dissenter turning up, all the old tales brought out and embellished, and Donald Norbrook himself among us. Four years later we did the same for the Silver Jubilee; Donald had died in the interim, so the stories were rather racier (like the cannabis plant which flourished for a period on his office windowsill while younger staff waited, breathless, to see whether he would notice). I doubt that the party will reassemble again: Andy Wright died, tragically young, at the turn of the millennium and I cannot imagine any of us having the heart to try and celebrate again, for he held the soul and conscience of the station in his hands. But it was a good time, and we have all acknowledged it, and that is the main thing.

Much of its quality was due to Donald Norbrook himself. I am not sure how vigorously the old boy led policy or actually determined the direction of the station, but I know that he defended us against Big BBC when we got into trouble. I also know that all of us younger ones somehow wanted to please him and not to fail by his standards; and I know that he had more of the true quality of a leader than many I have met in after years. One small example: during a period of intense IRA letter-bomb activity, when the BBC was specifically targeted, Donald quietly took to coming in an hour early, before the receptionist, and opening every single piece of post himself. 'Don't want Louise to be worried,' he would mutter, dropping envelopes everywhere and tutting at the odd bit of chewing-gum stuck to the reception desk. Then he would smile his sweet, crooked, edgy smile, and melt back into his office for the rest of the day.

I arrived in this world as innocent as Alice in Wonderland, armed only with a perfunctory training-course in how to work the local radio consoles. They were cute little things: their black faders were miniature versions of the big ones on older network desks, their technology all calculated to be worked with the minimum of staff. You could do everything remotely, provided you had quick hands, and with a hovering microphone on a stand over the desk you could do the talking as well. Thus you would — with a following wind — achieve all on your own the functions of a host of London staff: presenter, producer, studio manager, gram and tape player. You could cue and mix and talk, stop and start machines with your third hand, record yourself and later edit out the inevitable mistakes.

Unless, of course, it was live; in which case you just went down to the Dewdrop pub next door and got over your disaster in miserable privacy. Even so, the hot tide of shame ebbed quickly. Your colleagues would rib you, the programme organizer, Keith, would wince theatrically and flick his fingers, but there was just so much work to be done, so many broadcast hours to fill and link and pump out through the Beckley transmitter, that even the most appalling lapses were generally forgiven. It was a wonderful way to learn.

And, I repeat, it was also historically a very important period. It gave UK speech radio something which UK newspapers had had for generations: a provincial seed-bed for irreverent talent. By the time I left the station in 1977 it was evident that all over the national networks were reporters and presenters who had come through from the local stations of the early seventies bringing a straightforward unpompous manner and an insouciant attitude to risk-taking ('Give it a punt, it's only radio, and the audience quite like it when it goes wrong'). They brought back sharpness, freshness and informality to speech radio, qualities which had been gradually dulled since its early days.

At best, the local radio incomers learnt things in return from the old networks: thoroughness and sobriety and a less cavalier attitude to grammar and twisted bits of tape. But without their impetus, born of the energy and the fun of the local stations, it is possible that BBC network radio would have become quite dangerously moribund by now. Suppose it had? It could have lost much of its appeal except to the elderly, and been shunted into oblivion or sold to the record industry by Mrs Thatcher.

7

Painting with Sounds

In 1973, a young woman still had to put a certain amount of effort into being unfeminine. Shortly after I arrived, and re-learned the art of using the cripplingly heavy UHER 2000 tape machine, my reporting career resumed for the first time since *Tourist Trap*. Station assistants were not news reporters, and certainly not producers, but were expected to 'assist in providing material for sequence programmes' in addition to the usual announcing and operating duties. As I arrived a new strand was opening up, of fifteen-minute features in the afternoon. The edict went out that everyone on the station, bar the secretaries and engineers, had got to make one.

'Anything you want, anything about local life, whadd-you wanna do?' said one of the bustling young men. (There were no woman producers.) 'You could do the WI, p'raps. Or the playgroup movement, Angie's got some contacts through her National Childbirth people. Or something light and fun about — oh, beauty salons? Go on, what d'you want to do?'

I have never been particularly paranoid about female typecasting, but a warning bell rang in my head. Without a second's hesitation I did the Lady Macbeth mutter ('Unsex me here!') and said the most blokey thing which swam into my mind. I had been flat-hunting out in east Oxford because the condensation on the walls of the bedsit had gone beyond a joke. Remembering a sign I had seen, I said: 'I guess I'll do the stadium. Feature on the greyhounds, then maybe another one about speedway. OK?' It was a lucky shot. The station spent time in Cowley, but generally doing items on the history of Morris Motors or the modern British Leyland. As for sport, it covered mainstream football and cricket but had never stooped to consider the rather scruffy stadium and its regulars. The producer blinked.

'All right then. Do you know how to — er — set about it?'

'No sweat.'

I had no idea at all. But such was the dread of being transferred to an eternity of doing interviews on flower-arranging or maternity care that I hit the phones that very afternoon, and squeaked my breathless request. Before long I was spending every spare evening down at the track, being bought enormous drinks by men in sheepskin car-coats. ('Nah, go on, don' insult me asking for a Coke, darling — Stuart! Double brandy for the little lady!') I fraternized with dog-trainers and speedway kings, and tasted for the first time the heady pleasure of reportage. People claim all sorts of satisfactions for journalism, but I have always found that the greatest of them is the way that it enables a shy individual to horn in on alien lives and ask impertinent questions. I got on preposterously matey terms with people who, on the street, I would have edged past very nervously. I came back from my excursions glowing and full of bizarre new knowledge.

Even better, unlike a newspaper reporter with a mere notebook, I came back with tape. I carried home in my bag the people I had met — tough kids, ambitious trainers, injured speed kings, bragging wide-boys, bookies, sniffy bar-maids with views on the hoi-polloi. I had them imprisoned and preserved on brown tape, as exotic and glowing as butterflies on velvet. There is no pleasure to compare with the moment when you get back from your location, spool your tapes on to the big editing machine in the quiet of the evening, and listen again to your garnered treasures of character and wit, flavour and fact, sound and fury.

There are frustrations: hours spent 'de-umming', drifts of discarded woffle and 'er-ums' on the floor. There is the bad moment when you realize that fatigue has made you 'clean up' an interview so much that it now sounds unnatural, and must be stuck together again with some of the old 'ums' and hesitations, if only you can find the pieces. There is the awful moment when you discover that your wild-track of sound effects — the whizzing hare, the pattering dogs, the roaring crowd — has become mixed up with a passing aeroplane you did not hear at the time. There is the brutal disappointment of finding that because you did not watch the meter on the tape machine you have distorted and wrecked a beautiful unrepeatable interview with a rare character, or lost the moment when your hero exults in his first win all year, with the crowd roaring behind him and the bookie audibly saying, 'Oh, shit!'

Then, of course, there is the frowning debate with yourself over whether the 'Oh, shit!' is too audible, and will be vetoed by your producer to save Donald getting upset. And then there is the hardest bit of all: the cutting-to-length, where you have to throw away some of the very fades and mixes and effects you worked on with such care.

But I adored it. I loved, and still love, the rhythms of speech, and the way that a disembodied voice can get you closer to someone than a television picture ever could. Voices get into your head, and connect with you on a deep, human, emotional level. I was high on this new game and loved to play the human pipe-organ of sound and speech: I loved to aim at our invisible listeners a symphony of fading and juxtaposing, jokes and surprises and wake-up blasts of sound effects, offering them the illusion of having been beside me at the stadium. I suppose I felt — for the first time ever — a little like an artist. My personal history was once again reliving the history of the medium: some of the greatest adventures of radio's high days were Ewen McColl's radio ballads, with Peggy Seeger and the great producer Charles Parker. Before that, the palm belonged to the *Scrapbook* series, in which radio finally found the voices of the common people, and rejoiced in them.

Luckily, I have lost my two stadium documentaries now. I need not play them back and risk discovering that I was really just making rather mediocre plodding local radio features, and linking them in a somewhat squeaky voice. The sacred memory can remain intact.

But I do know that whatever they were, they cannot have been wholly incompetent, boring or jerky. They would not have got past Andy Wright if they had been. Radio Oxford feature standards were amazingly high, and this was largely due to him. Andy was a slight, spiky, stooping, bespectacled young producer with, to any cruel outside eye, the word 'geek' written all over him. It is to the credit of pretty Sally Bourdillon that she saw through this disguise instantly, spotted that he was Superman underneath, and nabbed him as a husband. Andy had been in at the launch of the first wave of stations and came to Oxford as a senior producer, and he was a craft genius. Better than that, he was a craft genius with a knife-like intelligence, a sharp sense of humour and a profound, well-concealed human sensibility. He loved the voices on the tape as much as I did; years more experienced, he felt the same thrill.

Three or four times in any media career you get the luck to work with somebody in whom talent and taste meet a passion for perfection, and who considers no trouble too great to make a feature better, even at two o'clock in the morning. If you are really, really lucky you meet one whose private ambition is modest, and who also likes to pass on the ability to others, so that

107

everything the station or network does will be as good as it can be.

They are quite tiring, these geniuses, and it is probably better to meet them when you are in your apprenticeship and don't have a family to get home to. Andy thought that if you were going to get something right, it didn't matter how long it took. It was not really his job to spend hours and hours training a new, green station assistant: but seeing that I wanted to learn, he was willing to teach. He would sit down with me, listen through the feature, smile sometimes, frown often, and then tell me with wounding clarity which bits were boring or in the wrong order. Or else he would dive into his special boxes and bring out some wonderfully rare little piece of music which would just add the finishing touch. Sometimes he would demand to hear the original tapes, divining that I had cut out a good bit.

A small example: I interviewed a professional toastmaster once, and got the chap to demonstrate his 'My Lords Laydeez and Gentlemen' at full blast. When he had finished, the toastmaster paused while the echoes died then said in a rather smaller (and somewhat camp) voice, 'Was that all right?' In my naiveté I cut off the last bit. Andy, who had been unhappy with the ending, scuffled on the floor looking for more atmosphere to fade into a record, found the relevant length of tape and spliced it back in. When he heard the shy little bleat of 'Was that all right?' he grinned and said, 'Yesss!'

Later, hearing it on the air, I understood what

he meant. It was a magical, unforced, glorious little radio moment; and I had not spotted it.

Gradually, I learnt to spot them even as they were happening, and this led to another torture: that heart-hammeringly terrifying moment when somebody is talking or singing or working quite beautifully, and you dare not distract them by glancing down to check whether the reels of your tape machine are actually going round. This happened when I was sitting at a vintage loom, kept for 'relaxation' by Richard Early of the famous Witney carpet factory. The old man decided to show me some old-style weaving, and began the satisfying business of shuttle-throwing and pedalling, with a lovely rattle. And then, with a sly, shy sidelong glance he began to sing in a high quavering voice:

I am a bachelor, I live with my son
  (swoosh, rattle!)
And we work at the weaver's trade (jigata-jig!)
And the only only thing that I ever did wrong swoosh!
Was to woo a fair young maid . . . (rattt-a-ta-tattt, swoosh!)

A TV documentary crew would probably have got him to do it three or four times until it became stagey. The radio way was to be quick and careful, to capture a real moment and take it home rejoicing.

I was soon allowed to do a series for the morning programme, jauntily entitled *Just the*

Job! These were five-minute cameos of a job or trade, mainly manual, and suited my new mood of exploration perfectly. I went to an Oxford building site — the heart of what is now the Westgate shopping mall near the railway station — and blagged permission to interview the crane driver about his life and feelings, explaining that it was essential for 'atmosphere' that I should do it in the cab of the tower crane, 120 feet up.

After a lot of to-ing and fro-ing about insurance (did they not understand that all twenty-three-year-olds are *ipso facto* immortal?) I got permission, and then realized with a sickening lurch of my stomach that I actually had to go up the thing. This is the trouble with journalism, whether radio, print or photographic, as any foreign correspondent will confirm. You get so wrapped up in the bureaucratic chase of getting permission for some excursion that you forget to be frightened until it is too late. My heavy tape machine sawing into my shoulder, my knees knocking, I realized that it was entirely impossible for me to get up the bloody iron ladder which stretched to infinity above me. I have always hated heights. My legs twitch and tremble with panic.

It was the men on the building site who saved me. They were mainly chippies, who apparently are famous for not liking heights themselves and thinking crane drivers mad. When I got near the foot of the machine they began barracking. *'You'll never get up there, luv.' 'Go home, do yourself a favour.' 'Whoooarrr! Seems a shame to turn that nice arse into strawberry jam!'* I stiffened up, and set my foot on the first rung. Then the next, then the next. Ten minutes later, at the top, gasping and trying not to cry, I pushed the heavy tape recorder ahead of me and made my way round the edge of the platform. This is the very, very worst bit; just as edging round the futtock-shrouds is the worst bit of climbing the rigging on a tall ship. My head swam; the sky above me suddenly seemed to be a floor far below me; I clung on to the rusting rail for a moment with eyes shut, then took the driver's hand and was hauled round to stand, quaking, on his platform. The men below were pasty dots amid the rubble; my city of Oxford lay around me, spires soaring triumphantly against a cyan sky.

The interview itself, inside the cab, was quite a sweet, melancholy affair. Crane drivers lead a lonely life (you can see why the famous Scunthorpe DJ chose to wear cowboy kit to keep his spirits up). This one was a nice young lad, and observed at one point that as his crane overlooked the yard of Oxford jail, he often felt sorry for the guys on exercise there. 'I could get the bucket down, pick a few up, over the wall, know what I mean?' Sadly, they made me cut that bit out, lest the Home Office take fright and stop the building work.

In the steamy little cab far above the world the interview went on, and on, and on because I was scared of climbing down again, especially the bit round the platform. Eventually the lad saw through my tactic and said, 'Shall I send you down in the bucket, then?' which shamed me

111

into climbing down. I half-expected a round of applause from the chippies on the ground, but they avoided my eye and ignored me as I left the site.

There were a score of other jobs in the series. I spent a day working with some removal men, got up at dawn to unblock grease-traps and climb down manholes with the sewermen, had a chaotic morning assisting some sheep-shearers, sat beside a patient, careful man who hand-rolled expensive pen-nibs, and joined a veteran British Rail signalman as he strode around polishing his brass handles and mourning the fact that he would be sitting at a modern electronic console with no view the week after next.

I began to understand how rapidly the world of work was changing, and how endangered were manual craftsmen. Since I was learning to be one myself, with my knobs and chinagraphs and razor blades, I felt lucky. I spent a wonderful day with Leonard Soden the chimney-sweep ('Father and grandfather were sweeps, did all the big college chimbleys and the Randolph Hotel') and then went back a few months later to expand the five minutes into a full half-hour programme about his family tradition and craft, *Soden the Sweeps*.

I did the rounds with a postman ('Nice little fences, this street, you can hop sideways from number two to number twenty-two and save yourself a lot of steps. Number twenty-four's got a bloody pond there, though'). I went to the Beckley transmitter to meet the BBC engineers who ran it, and savoured the wonderfully maritime atmosphere which always hung round these places: ships' clocks, shifts called watches, even brass bells. The first BBC transmitter engineers, in Reith's time, had come out of the Navy because that was where chaps knew about radio: the tradition continued to leave its elegant traces, right up to the present privatization.

All this taught me a lot about work, and the pride that can be taken in the most cruel and unpromising trades. The way the signalman polished his brass, the care with which the sweep and the builder tidied up after themselves, the sheep-shearers' insistence on never missing a strand or cutting a sheep, the dogged, swaying meticulousness of the sorters aboard the night mail train — all were as educational as Andy Wright's insistence on finicky care over the editing of the tapes and the removal of clicks and rumbles. I learnt about lives, too: one man who sticks in my memory particularly was a Geordie railway linesman who had been trudging and hammering up and down the track for forty years, careful and sober and slow.

'Did you always,' I asked brightly, 'want to work on the railways?' The answer was no. 'I trained,' he said gently, 'as a court dressmaker. Then the Depression came . . . '

The new depression had not yet come to southern England, in the early seventies. Or at least, it was coming by stealth. I had been two years on Radio Oxford when I was sent out to do an interview with a worrying, hitherto unheard-of set of young people: nice, well-behaved seventeen-year-olds who had been a full year out of school and — gasp! — *never had a job at all*. It seems crazy now that we found this so astonishing, but I clearly remember a group of horrified colleagues gathering round as I edited the tape. Never had a job! Not even waitressing! The shame and bewilderment of the teenagers was palpable. Today, when it is not uncommon on such estates to find two generations who have no idea of what it is to work, I think of them often. They were the forerunners. I hope they got jobs in the end.

When my obsession with jobs had run its course, I began to indulge a parallel fascination with the things people do for fun. St Giles' Fair, which blocks up the centre of Oxford every autumn, introduced me to the world of showmen, and for a while I had so many acquaintances on the fairgrounds that I read their newspaper, *World's Fair*, on a regular basis. I was lucky in that the rest of the Radio Oxford staff had been through three St Giles' Fairs already, and were sick of it; so it fell to me to pull stunts like finding an octogenarian called Nan Davies and taking her to the top of the Big Wheel to compare old fairs and new. I covered the magnificent showmen's service held on the eve of the fair, with the vicar perched on the Golden Galloping Horses and the steam-organ blasting out 'The Day Thou Gavest Lord Is Ended'. I chatted to the dodgem boys about the niceties of their trade.

I next made a bewitching (to me) documentary about Romany gipsies, and was taught to cook a hedgehog; then I fell in with Cottle and Austen's circus, puttering off on the moped to find it camped in a field outside Witney. I got into considerable trouble with the engineers when a performing llama ate my microphone windshield, but one friendship later bore rich fruit for my reporting career. I met Barry Walls, the fakir and fire-eater at the circus, and bonded instantly. So during the winter of 1973/4, when Britain was on a three-day week and OPEC oil prices had hit the roof and caused fuel shortages, I was able to make my first real tabloid phone call. I rang him in his winter quarters, and the conversation went something like this:

'Barry — you know this fuel crisis?'

'Yeah.'

'It must be really hard on fire-eaters. Shortage of fuel. A lot of people won't have thought of that aspect.'

'Well, actually — '

I knew as well as he did that one bottle of aviation kerosene lasted him all year. But I pressed on, unscrupulous.

'I think a lot of people would be *really interested* in the problem you've got there, Barry. Especially with the Christmas performances coming up.'

He got it. He gave me a wonderfully plaintive interview about the problems of an honest fire-eater held to ransom by distant sheiks. It went out on our news magazine, was taken up by the *Today* programme in London, and ran in

115

several newspapers. Oh, the triumph! And all of it pure nonsense. I suppose it was the first time I knowingly brought the Corporation into disrepute.

But Oxfordshire did not need to rely on visiting showmen for amusement. I found there, as I have always found since, that if you look at it closely enough, any community is plum-studded with happy eccentricities and careful, obsessive artistry. I developed a love of those too often dismissed as 'anoraks': the bored Cowley car workers whose spare time is devoted to building perfect working scale models of fairground engines, the silver-bandsmen, the keepers of immaculate pigeon-lofts. I made a programme about racing pigeons, going to the trouble of travelling overnight to Beachy Head in a pigeon-lorry, and watching them released in the pearly dawn in a cloud of dust, shit and feathers, and (luckily for the medium of radio) a very satisfying clatter of shutters and flapping of wings.

I found that when a man or woman talks on their enthusiasm or explains an expertise, selfconsciousness falls away and the microphone is forgotten, so that a little nugget of human truth and human nature falls into your hands. Such moments are to be carefully and reverently passed on to the host of listening strangers. On the whole, I always preferred to listen and record, rather than adopt the giggly 'have-a-go' style of broadcasting which was coming to be expected of girls (I only climbed the crane and went down the sewer because that happened to

116

be where the action was). However, I came seriously unstuck when I talked myself into going potholing.

Again, as with the crane, the logistics were dreadfully complicated: the station engineers were worried about the tape machine, however much we padded it. The risk was either that it would be wrecked or soaked, or else that it would cause a spark which would explode cave gases. The engineers spent some time looking up the rules for taking recording equipment down coal-mines. I became so focused on persuading them it was OK that I forgot about the claustrophobia.

Actually, I had rather stupidly imagined that caving involves big arched beautiful caves; and that if you squeeze through a narrow hole it is only a brief inconvenience, necessary to get into some fine vaulted elvish kingdom. I did not know that what cavers really do is to squeeze through impossible cracks in order to get to even more impossible ones. When we stood at the edge of a thing called Swildon's Hole, in Wiltshire, and I saw that the first step was to creep under a stone like a centipede, I hesitated but felt too stupid to refuse. I briefly recorded a 'well, here we are' conversation with the leaders, and wriggled in.

The next five hours were indescribably dreadful. The light on my head kept going out when I banged against rocks, which was often; the dripping, menacing darkness appalled me; the rope-ladder to nowhere nearly finished me off; stalactites attacked me, my clothes were torn, my knees bleeding, my terror extreme. Cheery potholers alongside me kept encouragingly promising that we would 'soon reach Sump One', and be able to dive underwater beneath a rock ledge and out the other side. They thought this was an incentive. Every twenty minutes or so on the way down, I took out the microphone and recorded breathless, frightened bits of interview. If I had not had that job to do, I would have behaved even worse than I did.

After two hours I cracked and said I had to go back. Uncomplaining, the excellent potholers sent someone to go with me, and the nightmare repeated itself at even greater length than before. Sometimes I could no longer feel which way was up: every path we wriggled along on our stomachs was dark, rocky, dank, set at crazy angles. Finally, pushing up through yet another crack, I laid my cheek on a flat rock in the wet darkness and thought I could not go any further.

'Lift your head,' said my companion. 'Look along the light beam . . . ' So I did, and saw a stranger sight than any: a curious vertical jagged stalagmite formation branching off into dozens of impossibly thin spikes. I stared.

'It's a tree,' said the potholer, spluttering with mirth. 'We're out'. So we were; and it was already night. I did one last brief recording on to the machine, then climbed into my seat in the minibus and fell asleep. I woke up screaming: they had to shake me and say, 'You're out, it's over, you're not underground.' Next day my doctor said he had never seen bruising so extensive except in professional boxers. Back at the station I had to ask Andy Wright to delay the broadcast of this particular fifteen minutes for a while, because I could not bear to listen to the tapes. When I eventually put the programme together he listened, laughed in his spiky way, and went into one of his music-chests to produce an echoing old rendition of Paul Robeson singing 'It's dark as a dungeon, way down in the mine'.

I thought it was the most horrifying programme ever, and still prefer not to listen to it. One listener, however, wrote in to say that my gabbling terror was the funniest thing he had heard in years.

* * *

A community is studded with nuggets of history. Whenever a World War II thirtieth anniversary came up — D-day, Montecassino, Dunkirk, VE Day — I would summon another contact (who later became a considerable broadcaster himself), the soldierly Dennis Payne. He knew absolutely everyone on the ex-servicemen's network, and could rustle you up a brace of D-day veterans or Dunkirk troops in half an hour. We even found the printer who, in deadly secret, printed the invasion maps at the Oxford University Press.

But the most striking bit of history came when I had done a spell on one of the morning quizzes which Thomas Prag put out on the breakfast show. This was the *Archive Quiz*, and gave me an excuse to fossick around in the BBC Archives. I would find little clips and ask what they were (the commentary from the year the ball burst during the FA cup, the signature tune of *Happidrome*, Neville Chamberlain, that sort of thing). One week I played a little bit of commentary from the ceremony in 1939 at which the trumpets found in Tutankhamen's tomb were played, for the first and only time in modern history, before being re-entombed in a museum.

It ended on the strange, wild blare of the trumpets, and one of the correct answers which came in made us stare in amazement. It was from the young Army bugler who actually played those notes. We rushed him in, and he told us the story with dignity, explaining that he had never feared the Mummy's Curse because he had blown the trumpets with reverence, thinking all the while of the long-gone musicians who made and played them. He deserved his lap of honour, that old hussar.

They all did: all my beloved voices. I loved my recordings, my phantoms of the living caught on curling brown tape, transformed into jerks of the Peak Programme Meter, pulsed down cables to the transmitter and sent out by a miracle of physics to the wider world. Sometimes, plugging up the jackfield in the morning when it was my turn to open the station by sending squeaks of tone to Beckley and reading out the early bulletin and traffic news, I felt through my yawns a kind of religious radiance.

This was it: this was radio, the most magical

and humane invention of the century. Purified of the physical, it sent the essence of human beings out to comfort other human beings. Or, in the case of squeaky girl reporters stuck down potholes, to make them laugh like drains.

8

Live and Kicking

Technically, all this feature-making was only the frilly edge of my job. The shifts went on, with announcements to make, music to log, producers to assist. Some cursory attention was given to improving the microphone technique of station assistants, and sometimes the announcer David Dunhill was sent down by Local Radio HQ to give us the occasional re-tread. He was a gentle, thoughtful man whose central message was 'think about what you're saying'. His main dislike was not any particular accent or timbre, but lapses into meaningless sing-song, or emphasis put on irrelevant words, as in: 'The meeting *of* the council yester*day* . . . '

To cover weekends and early shifts I learnt to read the news straight off the teleprinter rip-and-read service, and discovered the pitfalls of such instant bulletins. Those in London who wrote them for the local radio service did not always bother to read them aloud. Try these — both real — and you will see what I mean:

The news reached Mr Macmillan on the golf course, where he was playing a round with Lady Dorothy . . .

Two soldiers were injured in Northern Ireland

last night, one in the Falls and one in the Bogside Area . . .

So I also learnt how you can stop yourself from corpsing in appalling, tasteless, irresistible laughter. It's simple. What you do is to throw your head back and stare at the ceiling. This stretches the throat muscles and makes laughing harder; and besides, a studio ceiling is a bland pale boring thing, and the sight of it calms you. Only you should not confide this secret to your colleagues, because they will Blu-Tak some hilarious sign to the ceiling above your microphone in the hope of making you lose control and topple backwards off the chair. At six o'clock on a grey, wet Oxford morning, one must take one's amusements where one can.

Sometimes, there was a bit of disc-jockeying to be done, at the homely level of the record request show *Home Choice*. I loved doing it. It was the opposite of the monkish, self-effacing business of making features: you had to get up there and smile and play the records and 'be yourself' — or at least a rather pleasanter version of yourself. If you made a hideous mistake, you had to laugh and apologize and soldier on regardless.

Just as literary writers enjoy flirting with newspaper deadlines and short-order commissions, even the most tape-drunken feature-makers get a buzz from going live on air from time to time. There is something immensely restful about knowing that once it is over there is nothing you can do to make the product better, except go to the pub and gild the memory with a few pints. 'Nooh . . . it wasn't that bad . . . ' you say, staunching your inward bleeding ' . . . listeners quite like it when things go wrong/you play a record at double speed/you hiccup.'

I relished my afternoons standing in for Sally on *Home Choice*, jigging to the music, practising fancy talkovers and whisking faders open and shut with debonair confidence. In my newfound affection for the local community I truly loved to say: ' . . . and this one's from Judy and Sam, to everyone at number thirty-five Botley Close — that's Mum, Dad, Granpa, Nanna, Duane, Marianne, Crazy Casey, baby Tracey and Sinatra-the-cat. And Judy and Sam tell me that you'd all love to hear Suzi Quatro's 'Can the Can' — so — heeeere we go!'

To do *Home Choice* was to wallow in a warm bath of simple human sentiment. Every 'sha-la-la-la', every 'wo-woo-woo-wo', every 'shing-a-ling-ling' and 'ooh, yeah' and moody arpeggio flowed over your skin like balm, especially if your own love-life was rubbish and your family far away. It was good even when you absolutely hated the record — and these were the 1970s, so there was a lot to hate. Osmonds were everywhere, yowling 'Puppy Love' and 'Long-haired Lover from Liverpool'. Clive Dunn's 'Grandad' was requested every single day. St Winifred's School Choir rampaged unchecked across the land and the Yellow Ribbon Round the Old Oak Tree showed no sign of ever being untied and used to garotte the composer. Never mind, I loved it all. But it was not my show but

Sally's, and she was a far nicer person than me and better at disguising her antipathy to the records from Hell.

On the other hand, she had a baby. So on Christmas Day, two years running, I had the job of opening the station all alone and doing the early record requests and good wishes to the region. That suited my Tiny Tim frame of mind very well indeed. Firemen and police and hospital workers on shift rang in with silly messages for each other; women struggling with the turkey rang up with rueful humour, and a crackling Dickensian bonhomie sprang up to comfort any loneliness there might have been out there. It was a privilege to be involved in the process. It made you feel as if you had a part in *It's a Wonderful Life*, as the kindly old druggist dispensing goodwill along Main Street UK. Besides, the Christmas records of the time were nonpareil: Slade and Wizzard and Lennon's heavy, ironic Liverpudlian tones turned gooey-peacenik with a chorus of children singing 'Happy Christmas, War is Over'.

Which, of course, it wasn't: there was a shooting war in Cyprus, a coup in Greece, the Middle East was in flames and Pol Pot was shelling Phnom Penh. For the moment, though, these were only lines on the rip-and-read news. I still had no particular urge towards heavy current affairs because I was too much in love with the barmy English diversity of my own immediate neighbourhood.

After a while, on the local radio principle that you work the willing horse until it drops, I got

125

my own book programme on Saturday mornings, daringly entitled *Review*. The Radio Oxford catchment area was jampacked with authors both learned and popular: from John Wain and John Jones to Miss Read, from Brian Aldiss to Johnny Morris. Besides, publishers were just starting to latch on to the existence of local radio and the importance of book tours to sales. Once I had explained that I was doing a real, Radio 4-ish live book programme they were more than willing to pay the fares of authors to come on the show. Several publicists have since confided that they deliberately sent people to me — handy, close to London, reasonably literate — as practice for the more terrifying national programme *Start the Week*. I pride myself on breaking-in a good few writers who later went on to chat their hearts out all over network radio, and we certainly gave plenty of established authors a quick practice session on how to talk about their latest book.

In the process I had a great deal of fun. How else does a callow twenty-four year old get to grill Brian Aldiss and James Blish together about the meaning of sci-fi, or gently take the mickey out of Shirley Conran's brand new *Superwoman* concept? One of my proudest moments was corpsing the duty station assistant when Ms Conran was discussing the use of Steradent to get the stains out of fine china. 'Even better, you could pop your teeth in the teapot overnight and kill two birds with one stone,' I said, as earnestly as I could, and beyond the glass panel saw the duty SA fall off his chair at the authoress's expression.

On the other hand, there were authors who even my respectful, tender and persistent interviewing could not manage to drag into the new age of book-media. One of the perennial unspoken truths about book programmes on radio and television is that some of the finest, subtlest writers become that way because they are frankly hopeless at expressing their thoughts and feelings in conversation. Meanwhile, plenty of brilliant conversationalists and beguilingly soundbitey interviewees write dreadful, plodding books. Only a few do both things properly. Yet because the media want chatty authors, chatty authors are the ones who get most publicity, most easily, while better writers go unpublicized. It is maddening.

One of my private missions in life was to get an inspiring interview out of the detective novelist Michael Innes. In real life he was a don, J. I. M. Stewart of Christ Church, and in my local radio years was writing a series of books under his own name, notably *Young Pattullo* and *The Gaudy*. They were brilliant; his detective stories too were subtle and excellent. Faithfully, I invited him in for every book; I read them with care, worked out my questions to create an easy, reflective atmosphere (so I thought), and struggled away in the little pre-record news studio, the most informal setting on the station. I really wanted to share the wonderfulness of Stewart with the listenership.

I never got *anywhere*. He replied in dry, dull,

short, non-committal sentences, interspersed with long silences and clearings of the throat. On the page this man sparkled with humanity and wisdom and humour. In private life his friends and family loved him dearly and sought his company. Across a microphone he was dire. And he knew it, and didn't seem to mind. At the end of the third interview, when our loose acquaintance had lasted just over two years, he gave me a seraphic smile as I wound back yet another terrible tape, and said: 'Well, you didn't get much change out of the old boy that time, did you?'

★   ★   ★

Even more stimulating than live broadcasting in the studio is doing it out of doors. I managed to weasel my way into all the outside broadcasts I could, even when it meant feigning an interest in sport. At Henley Regatta I went live on-air amid the boatered crowds in the Royal Enclosure, and had the heady experience of getting four rude words on the BBC in one sentence when a public-school type responded to my question about the music with the words: 'Band's a bloody nuisance actually, last night I went arse over tit over one of their trombones in the bog.'

I also had immense live fun on a Sunday for a while, learning just how nimble radio can be by helping out on a programme called *Sunday Joint*. Thomas Prag sat demurely in the studio playing the records while I went out in the radio car with Henry Aubrey-Fletcher, a local farming swell and old Etonian, to do live inserts from some event which had taken our fancy. We whooped and prattled away from the scene of seventeenth-century battle reconstructions, gymkhanas, adventure playgrounds, fêtes, horse shows, stately homes, swimming galas, zoos, tug-o'-war competitions and folk nonsenses like dwile flunking. We pounced on anybody remotely interesting for quickfire interviews.

It was while doing *Sunday Joint* on a riverbank with a particularly garrulous angler that I discovered a secret of live broadcasting that has served me very well on other occasions, notably during the Royal Wedding. It is only available to radio broadcasters, not TV, and it goes like this: if your interviewee won't draw breath or end his interminable sentence, and is impervious to your 'wind-up' gestures and grimaces while the studio is bellowing in your ear to hand back, there is one thing which the radio reporter can do without interrupting and sounding rude. You just reach out and touch the speaker, preferably on bare flesh.

It can be anywhere at all — the arm will do — but for the repressed British, the shock of physical contact with a stranger will cause a brief faltering which will enable you to say, 'Well, Sam Bumble, that's fantastic. Thanks for talking to us. Back to Tom in the studio — who I bet has *never* caught a fifty-two-pound pike!'

Then you can make your peace with the interviewee off-air. Only don't try this flesh-touching thing with a Frenchman or a Spaniard. They touch back, gripping your hand fondly with many a suggestive squeeze, and bloody well carry on talking.

Henry Aubrey-Fletcher was technically minded, and owned a great deal of secret and unlicensed equipment which made our lives much easier. In particular he had a radio microphone, an unheard-of luxury in local radio in the seventies. We were supposed to do interviews near the radio car by unreeling great drums of cable and somehow stopping people falling over it, but Henry short-circuited this system by bringing his own unauthorized radio mike and feeding its output into the car console. He also invented an even more illegal talkback system we evasively called 'magic', whereby the person in the car could transmit instructions to an ordinary FM set which the roaming reporter two fields away was carrying to hear the live studio cues.

I am almost sure that our noble and law-abiding station engineers know about this now; otherwise this constitutes a formal confession. Sorry, Cliff. Sorry, Derek. We know it would have been more than your job was worth. We confess that it was not BBC-approved equipment and that 'magic' was unlicensed VHF. But it made it a great deal easier to broadcast live from assault courses and abseils, and gave much innocent pleasure. Henry was pleasingly cavalier about his precious toy, and on one occasion handed the radio mike to a boy of ten and ordered him to do the commentary — live — while Henry tried to swing across a river on a rope. The child was brilliant.

The only problem was that when Henry wandered off with the radio mike and I was left in charge of the car, I could not reel him back on the cable-drum or find him by following the wire. All I could do was yell down the illegal talkback, 'Where are you, for God's sake? Tom wants us on in thirty seconds and he wants to know where you are!' and get a cheeky reply along the lines of, 'Hahaaa, wait and see!' Shortly afterwards I would hear Henry saying, on-air, 'I'm on an elephant, with a lady in hardly any clothes.'

Thomas was very calm about it. I was not a bit surprised when in after years he won all his Sony Awards.

The other memorable outside broadcast I did was May Morning. Every year since the station was founded, Humphrey Carpenter had done a commentary on May 1st from 5.30 a.m., live from the top of Magdalen College Tower. By long tradition the choir sing a hymn at 6, *Te Deum Patrem Colimus*, the old College Grace; they take their note from the last stroke of the clock. After the hymn the crowd disperses to fall in the river or frolic through the May morning streets in floral hats, welcoming the summer.

In recent years the event has been coarsened by longer pub hours and yahoo behaviour, and the college has taken to relaying the hymn through loudspeakers, so nobody has to bother keeping quiet. When Humphrey covered it, though, it was all done the old way. The silence still held the revellers on the bridge, as people craned raptly to catch a few, falling notes as if

131

they were a blessing. It was impractical — often enough they would be snatched away by the wind or drowned by a passing aeroplane — but it was rather beautiful.

One year, shortly before he moved on, Humphrey decided not to do Mayday any more, and informed the programme organizer that he was passing it on to me. I do not know why. There were plenty of more senior people, and I had never done any kind of live commentary. Humf, however, was adamant. He gave me his historical notes and told me to write and improvise my own script. So for three Maydays I had the inestimable privilege and unbeatable fun of helping the engineers rig long cables up the tower and tune the radio car the day before, then being let in through the Magdalen fortress doors at 4.30, climbing the tower with the flapping, excited boy choristers, and conducting a live commentary on the dawn, with interviews as the children lined up, timing it all to fall silent just before the clock began to strike (the engineers issued dire warnings that if the silence was too long, the transmitter would switch itself off, so it was a fine judgement).

Like *Sunday Joint*, it gave me a taste for outside broadcasts which I have never shaken off. Who needs a studio chair when you can perch on some unsafe medieval leading? Who needs sound-effects records when there are real birds swooping and chirping round the pinnacles in the still dawn? Who can get a buzz out of a safe, controlled, sound-insulated environment after grappling with the unpredictability of the outer world, with nothing but your microphone in one hand and an FM radio in the other providing a cue from the studio?

Once, turning rather sharply from a soliloquy on the pink dawn over Shotover to interview the organist, I stuck the FM aerial up my nose by accident and developed a spectacular Hammer House of Horror nosebleed. No option: I had to keep on talking while the blood ran down my coat. The choirmaster kept an admirably straight face as he talked reverently about the morning's second anthem, but the boys behind him were laughing so hard that they could barely get the first note out when, eventually, I wound up just after 0559.

I was not paid for much of this. Extra Responsibility Reward (ERR in Beebspeak) was scarce in local radio, budgets tight. The loose assumption on which stations like Oxford had to survive was that station assistants who went beyond their duties did so as volunteer members of the host community. I was not bothered: unmarried, boyfriendless, perfectly content in my scruffy student wardrobe, charmed by my job, paying a low rent for a shared house with a brace of young teachers and a trainee kidney machine technician, I failed to notice the galloping inflation of the period. I genuinely needed no more money than I had. But others in my position elsewhere in the country, with heavier responsibilities and longer service, were up in arms at this exploitation of the willing operator-grades. The unions told the BBC that station assistants must be paid properly for their extra work.

The result was instant and inevitable: the work was taken away. One month I was doing a great deal of production, presenting, interviewing and feature-making on top of my proper work. The next, I was not. I was a bored, underemployed drone, watching overworked producers trying to fill the gaps left by the likes of me.

After a miserable few weeks of this I demanded an interview with my personnel officer in London and travelled up, feeling rather odd about coming once more under the shadow of Broadcasting House. She listened to my exposition of the problem — that I was shrieking bored and frustrated at not being allowed to stretch my wings any more — and then cocked her head on one side and began to ask gentle, caring questions.

Did something else lie behind this discontent? Was I involved, perhaps, in an unhappy relationship with someone on my station? Someone senior, perhaps? It was safe to tell her, she could arrange a transfer and perhaps counselling . . .

I almost screamed at the impertinent, patronizing sexism of it. Just because I was a young woman, how dare this skinny witch assume that any problem I had was romantic? Cow! I left, brooding. As it happened, the brief panic about the budget subsided shortly afterwards, and I went back to doing more or less the job I had done before, and even being paid a bit extra. But the writing was on the wall. I realized that life was not, after all, just a matter of enjoying the moment and trying to do everything better every day. Systems and bureaucracies, too often run by fools, will in the end blow so much sand at you that you will suffocate. I would have to think constructively about where my working life was leading. There would plainly be no producer jobs at Oxford for years — everyone was too contented — so I had to think of something else. In the end, I decided with some reluctance that I ought to try and work in news for a spell.

I was not a natural newshound. Once, riding my shaky moped down the road at dawn for the 6 a.m. shift, I noticed three fire-engines parked outside my local garage. I failed to glance up (well, in my defence, let me point out that my helmet had a long peaked eyeshade) and merely thought, 'Hmm, I suppose fire engines have to get diesel somewhere, funny time of day to do it though.' When I got in, I found that the top story was a vast blaze which had gutted the garage and left nothing of it intact above 10 feet. Which is to say, above my helmet-peak viewing level.

Nor was I especially engaged with the national and international news. It was pure pleasure for a former sixties student to be on duty in 1973 to announce the Vietnam ceasefire, certainly; and as for the national emergency of the time, we read out the times of rota power cuts in the three-day week. But I was not very news-literate. Local news was more immediate: the endless wildcat strikes at British Leyland affected all of us, and indeed the workers often trusted local radio to deliver their point of view, so we got plenty of informal little scoops (it helped if in the previous week you had been doing interviews with the winner of the Morris Motors Athletic and Social Club Cage Birds Section Annual Canary Championship. I think they realized that we saw them as rounded people, not just cartoon strikers).

Later on, in the summer of the Great Drought, the local water news was to become bracingly relevant, and we ran a ridiculous feature called *Droughtline*, in which officials from Thames Water came on and offered interesting new ways to economize on water ('Only wash the naughty bits,' said their house doctor once, causing Mike Dickin to corpse horribly). Actually, that interlude had contributed to my dislike of corporate establishments. Having gone round ordinary homes for months as a reporter, seeing how loyally and patriotically Oxfordshire people were flushing the lavatory with bathwater and keeping plants alive with vegetable-water, I was enraged when the reservoirs were brimming in the autumn, yet the water company still refused to withdraw their pleas for economy and tell these honest people it was all right to flush after a wee again. If you ask citizens for co-operation in a crisis, the least you can do is thank them and stand them down when it's over. If it were left to some public authorities, we would still be saving scrap metal to build Spitfires and blacking out the windows at night, just in case.

But in general, news was not my first choice of a career. The only reason I applied for a news attachment was that I clearly had to start moving on, and it was the only one on the board (apart from a sports attachment: in a moment of bravura I applied for that too, and valiantly pretended to understand rugby all through an interview with Cliff Morgan, but thought better of it).

Eventually I was summoned to be considered for six months as a trainee producer on the Radio 4 *Today* programme. The interview was in autumn 1974, and on the night before it, I got back from a newspaperless holiday in Ireland to stay with my very political, very adult friend Miranda.

She mentioned someone called 'President Ford' and I said: 'President Ford of where?' It didn't sound French or German.

'Of the United States of America, fool,' said Miranda.

'No, no, that's Nixon. You know, the Watergate one.'

She sighed. 'He resigned a month ago. This is a news attachment you're being interviewed for, did you say?'

'Shit!'

So Miranda gave me a brief tutorial in world affairs, and somehow or other I talked my way in, and cut a deal to stay in her flat for six months and be a London bird again.

9

Into Newsland

It was only a six-month attachment, but a very interesting time to arrive. *Today* had recently lost Robert Robinson, and gone through a phase of trying out a succession of presenters to replace him alongside the ever-faithful, ever-jovial (well, at least on air) John Timpson. There was, as yet, no breakfast television to compete with; *Today's* success under Robinson and Timpson had eased it into public consciousness as the favoured morning listening of the ruling establishment. So it had glamour enough to entice the big names to try out as presenters: James Burke, Malcolm Billings, Barry Norman, even Melvyn Bragg had a go. John Timpson, in his book *Today and Yesterday*, drily observed, 'Melvyn Bragg, once described to me as Robert Robinson in paperback, came and rapidly went.'

However, presenting *Today* did not suit everyone. The hours finished off a few, the atmosphere and the tension of fast news work got others down. Many relaxed, evening-style broadcasters simply sounded wrong first thing in the morning. By the time I got there, John Timpson's regular partners were Barry Norman and the sports reporter Desmond Lynam, who later became a TV sport anchorman and mysterious object of desire for the women of middle England (who appear to be a pushover for a bristly moustache and a terminally relaxed manner).

But frankly, the presenters didn't matter all that much to us on the production team. Hell, they were just people who turned up in the morning and linked the items which we had painstakingly assembled for them over the previous twenty hours. We gave them their cue to each tape, neatly typed out, so that they could re-write it in their own voice. We briefed them in close detail for the live interviews (rather fewer in those days). We set the running order, timed it to the second and snapped instructions down the talkback to cut things short, ask the question again, or wind up instantly and cue Thought for the Day. We told them when to pad for a minute with a 'ho-ho' (a funny line out of the morning papers usually) if a newsreader or sports reporter had fallen over the breakfast-trolley or got locked in the gents.

The presenters were out there, starring, but we in the backroom team controlled them. Having been both sides of the glass in my time, I am aware that the relationship probably looked different to John, Barry and Des. They may even have deluded themselves into believing that we were working *for* them, not working them. But network presenters, you may be surprised and shocked to hear, do not always enjoy the reverent admiration of their production teams. The machine of a sequence news programme is very big, and the bit of it the presenter operates is — though impressive to the listener — actually not the most important. Happy, sensible presenters understand this. Chippy, self-important ones do not, and are a pain in the neck.

The presenters of the seventies were far softer, in news terms, than they are today. In recent years we have grown accustomed to having hard-nosed and combative news addicts like John Humphrys and James Naughtie as *Today* presenters: it was not always so. There were some politically keen and intellectual reporters on the programme, notably Robert Fox, but the presenters, bright as they were, came from a different stable. Barry Norman was more of a film-and-feature man than a politico. Des Lynam's heart was still at the sportsdesk. Nor was John Timpson himself a passionate political animal. He had been a cub reporter and a newspaperman, but his favourite job at the BBC before *Today* was Court Correspondent — and this was in the dear dead days of deference, when a sprightly aside about the Duchess of Kent's décolleté was about as daring as you got. On *Today* John Timpson was a confident, jovial ringmaster who introduced the acts and conducted interviews with style, aplomb and reasonable gravitas, but none of the farouche passion or aggression of the modern programme. Above all he was a Presence: a jocose, good-tempered sound to wake up to.

With such a team — with any team, indeed — producers and day editors were essential guides: not quite puppetmasters but a vital substructure without which the presenters could have made ripe old fools of themselves.

I was a trainee producer, not meant to do interviews and confined to one big room full of telephones. It was a far narrower job specification than I was used to, and I resignedly expected to fizz with frustration after the liberty of local radio. But to my surprise I enjoyed the invisible role of cog in a big machine. I liked research, the terrierish pursuit of a story by telephone, cuttings and reference-book; and while at times I wished I was on a newspaper and could just write down what I had learned, I came to relish the radio-maker's dilemma of finding speakers to explain and illustrate it in their own voice.

I even liked briefing reporters, most of whom were serious newsmen and a joy to deal with. The few who decided to be haughty and dismissive of a young female trainee producer provided a quite different satisfaction, because whether they liked it or not, we stood between them and their adoring public. We edited their interviews. Give the young producer any grief, boys, and she will cruelly get her revenge by taking out all your hyper-clever questions, and especially removing the bits where the minister says, 'That's a very good question, and not a lot of people think to ask it.'

As for the presenters, I liked writing amusing or dramatic cues, in the distinctive 'voice' of each, and seeing whether in the morning they would fall for the trick and use my witty words unchanged, or whether their *amour-propre* and professional pride would make them turn the

141

whole thing on its head.

Above all, I liked my new colleagues — a cheerful, slightly ramshackle bunch. The team which gathered round that vast cluttered table in the *Today* office had a certain loopy, tribal ensemble quality which I have rarely seen elsewhere (outside, that is, the TV comedy Drop the Dead Donkey, which years later made me stare in astonishment at how well they had caught the atmosphere). The usual office feuds and tensions simmered, the usual flirtations flared and failed, but it went beyond that. Because of the odd working hours our inhibitions were loosened, and it was a place where character flowered freely and comically. Fond memories return: the epically rude PA telling a listener on the phone not to be so bloody thick; or the aspiring Tory MP, who as a reporter did immaculately balanced tapes but then left them for us with cues along the lines of, *'For six weeks now the honest people of Glasgow have suffered the mounting horror of uncollected rubbish while their dustmen indulge themselves in industrial action.'* Or David Mellor (not the ex-minister, nor the cutlery man, but another chap entirely) amusing the whole office with stagey phone calls as he tried to set up interviews. *'Oh, dear, Mr Whitelaw, I'm sorry to have got you out of the bath. Yes, especially when you'd just got in . . . '*

There was a definite *Today* type, within a department which also offered the choice of the *World at One* and the *PM* programme. Some people gravitated towards the early-morning show because they simply felt freer working through the small hours, without any management in the building. When senior management did drop in at 1 a.m. it was generally after a very good dinner so they were nice and mellow. On at least one occasion the dinner was so good that the night duty editor Martin Cox got a slurred phone call at 2 a.m. summoning him to Paddington Green Police Station to bail out an executive who had swung a punch at the guard after missing his last train home. 'He borrowed my tie for his court appearance in the morning, too,' says Martin plaintively. 'I never got it back.'

Some came to *Today* primarily because they liked the buzz of ushering in the nation's morning, breaking world stories to Britain. Some appreciated the double satisfaction of having both a big audience and so much time to fill that there was plenty of room for quirky, inessential, amusing items about phantom puma sightings or people who played tunes by hitting themselves on the head with spanners. Some just liked the shifts which, though bizarre, opened up the opportunity to live far out of town, in one case as far away as Wales. Some led double lives. Jolyon Monson, a duty editor, actually ran a smallholding and used to bring in new-laid eggs speckled with straw and authentic chicken-shit, to sell to the rest of us in the office.

The shifts certainly were remarkable. Sometimes you worked a quite reasonable week of three twelve-hour shifts — nine till nine, I think it was — but when I arrived a fairly short-lived experiment was under way in which both the day editor and the producer who ran the studio in the morning worked only two shifts a week. Each of those shifts was twenty-two hours long.

Yes, twenty-two hours. You came in at noon, and were on duty until ten the next morning, after a handover meeting with the day staff and a restorative office breakfast of Marmite toast and neat whisky. The idea was that a core team of two should be responsible for one programme all the way — from its very beginnings the day before, until its final goodbye on-air. This system evolved because of the corrosive bitterness which always develops between night and day teams, and the chippiness of the handover system. In an extension of the classic engineer's surly growl of 'It's all right leaving me . . . ', day and overnight teams are always prone to accuse one another of wrecking the show.

'I left them some bloody good material, and it never made the air, and they used that pillock's interview instead.'

'Frankly, with the crap the day team left us it's a miracle we filled the programme at all . . . ' etc.

To prevent this, someone — possibly the tall, languid editor Alistair Osborne, who would never have to work it — invented the twenty-two-hour shift. The same editor and producer who shambled in at 10 a.m. on Sunday would go right through to directing the programme on Monday dawn. Then they would go home and fall into a troubled sleep before returning on Wednesday to do the same thing again; and that was their week over. They could sleep it off and have three days to regain normal

144

control of their eyeballs.

Once I had been there a month or so I was considered fit to do the long producer shift — which included the nerve-racking business of directing the programme minute-by-minute in the studio from 6.30 to 9 while the editor, high on adrenalin but fogged with exhaustion, whizzed in and out changing the order of things, booking unexpected two-ways with Nicaragua and generally rotting up your arrangements and making your presenters even more nervous and snappy than usual.

It was a strange, strange life on that shift. You came in and worked through the day, having conferences, reading the morning papers, then gutting the two London evening papers for more ideas, and groaning when the *World at One* or *PM* shot your fox by bagging a story you were hoping they would not notice. You made suggestions, frowned over other people's, and endlessly telephoned to research stories or to book interviewees. Holding a phone to your ear for hours on end can cause actual pain: red, swollen lobes as you tensely press it to your head saying: 'Yes . . . yes, I see that — but our problem is we need somebody to put the other point of view . . . no, we could arrange a taxi — well, it could be done tonight if you like, from the Durham studio — '

Then there would be a panicky rush to book the studio, book the line, book the taxi and shunt a spare reporter in to do the interview, first holding him down for five minutes while you hammered the briefing into his head.

We were not supposed, as producers, to do any interviewing ourselves. Once or twice that rule was broken in sheer exasperation by a former local radio jack-of-all-trades like me. On one occasion my brother Mike, who picks up all sorts of silly stories in City bars, rang to say that he had been drinking with an advertising man who had just done a deal selling poster-space on the flanks of cows alongside the London to Brighton line. The cows were to be living hoardings, wearing coats marked SMIRNOFF VODKA.

As a veteran of stories about fire-eaters suffering from petrol shortages, I saw the potential in this for cheering up the nation on a grey morning, sold the idea to the day editor and booked the ad-man to come into the studio. However, the duty reporter rebelled. He was a heavy, portentous young man, seconded to us from the Newsroom and rather sniffy at not yet being made a Serious Correspondent. He was also smarting with irritation at my having spitefully removed a 'Very perceptive question, if I may say so' from his interview with the Home Secretary a few days earlier. He said flatly that he was too busy 'preparing' for his important interview with some important bore, and that he was not hired to do 'froth'.

So I did it myself, back in the interviewer's seat at last, and was very happy when the newspapers picked it up and ran it later in the week. One of the perennial irritations for me was the way that radio news magazines — being less resourced — were always following the newspapers. It bred a bad habit of timidity, in which nobody was prepared to do a story unless there was a black-and-white cutting in his hand. On another occasion brother Mike — who worked on *Fishing News* — tipped me off that there were fishermen in Cornwall selling their catch at sea direct to Russian factory ships because domestic prices were so low. *Today* wouldn't do the story when I gave them all the contacts; a month later the *Evening Standard* splashed it, and only then did we follow it up. I sulked all afternoon. For I had, by this time, caught the news bug.

So anyway, that was your working day. By eight or nine o'clock at night you felt you had put in your time; but on the twenty-two-hour shift there were still thirteen hours to go.

Through the evening your vitality took a dip; there were dozens of tapes to edit, and now it was the plastic headphones that began to hurt your throbbing ears. Sometimes, sleepily, you dropped a whole sentence on the floor, a curling brown lock of tape, and had to scramble around desperately for the one vital point that Denis Healey, Merlyn Rees or Clive Jenkins had made, before somebody trod on it and crumpled it up or stretched it so that the voice went wobbly. All the time you had to maintain a sense of balance and fairness, not unfairly editing out any nuance of meaning or betraying the context of a remark. If it was 'actuality' of a lively industrial story or a local dispute, you had to weigh up how many swear-words to leave in. There had been a famous uproar in 1970 when Peter Sellers, in an interview, said that he had 'pissed himself with

147

laughter' working with Goldie Hawn. Things had eased up a bit under the wise diktat of the Managing Director of Radio, Aubrey Singer. Rather charmingly, he put out an informal edict on words such as 'fucking' and 'bloody' which said: 'If these words sometimes come up naturally in the heat of the moment, fine. But I will not have people sitting down and *typing them out*.' It remains, in my view, the best guideline for rude words on radio.

When your editing was under control, you went off for half an hour for supper in the canteen, and relaxed. Sometimes, on a very quiet night, you even went out to a restaurant nearby and tried very hard to refrain from drinking anything to wash down your *Pollo Sorpresa*. ITN used the same restaurant, so that if the editor had a friend or two there you might pick up a story or a contact which had dropped off the bottom of their ten o'clock bulletin.

And then you went back to work. At 11.30 or so the next day's papers came in, causing another scramble, and the Far Eastern time zones would begin emitting news of battle or disaster. If there was an interview to be conducted down the line from the other hemisphere, one of the few remaining reporters had to be found (possibly asleep in a cuddy off the Newsroom with the *Economist* over his face) and prodded into wakefulness. Sometimes, just for a laugh, late at night we would ring the Presidential palace in Uganda and talk to the batty and insomniac tyrant Idi Amin. He would answer the phone and pretend it was not him, but it nearly always was.

Every half hour or so you would wander to the teleprinters to see if any fresh news was coming in, something to brighten up the programme in the morning. Inevitably, wars and disasters were most of it. I became a little anxious at the way my own shell of callousness grew: at first I was horrified by tales of massacre and misery, and some nights the whole world seemed to smell of death. I particularly remember editing sound from a fire-bombed building in Germany with distinct cries of 'Hilfe, Hilfe' from the dying on the upper floors; colleagues seemed impervious to the horror, but I had lived in Germany for a while, and it was as vivid to me as an English voice crying 'Help!'

On another night a tape was passed to us by the police, from a man claiming to have strangled the heiress Lesley Whittle whose body was found in a drain shaft; they thought it might be running at the wrong speed, hampering identification, so I was sent to adjust it on a variable speed machine. For two hours I worked on the man's gloating, grating voice. He was, as it turned out, a hoaxer, but I did not enjoy my long midnight intimacy with him. The voice, divorced from the body, is a frighteningly intimate route into a person's soul. That is one of the strengths of radio, but can be one of its stresses.

Gradually I got used to it and rather welcomed dreadful, distant developments as grist to the news mill. I tried not to. Once, I

149

wrote an angry poem about a night shift, ending
with the words:

With any luck Pnomh Penh
Will fall by 0810.

Satirical though it was at our expense, I felt
ashamed of it twenty-five years later when I met
one of the orphaned survivors of Cambodia and
confronted the reality of her terrible childhood.
But how, how can you truly care about everyone,
everywhere, when you are exhausted and hyper,
stressed and giggly and three-quarters asleep
after eighteen hours of a shift which still has four
to go?

The one night when I did almost collapse in
waking nightmare was when they were working
to extract corpses from the Underground after
the Moorgate disaster. Horrible reports — many
far too horrible to broadcast — were brought in
by our reporters, and I had not been able to
contact my eldest brother, who worked in the
City area, for two days. In fact he had gone off
on some diving jaunt, but in the fog of
exhaustion I convinced myself that he was in
the wreckage. The only light relief came when
one of our daffier reporters got back patting his
pockets and saying, 'Oh, damn — lost my
notebook. I remember . . . I took it out to get
the spare mike out of my pocket and put it on
this table. Never mind, it had my name and
address on it.'

There was a silence in the office. Then: 'Dave
— what table?'

'Oh, there was a table. With some other wallets and stuff on it.'

'That,' said the editor, 'will have been the possessions taken from the dead. By this time you will be on the list. Do you think you had better ring your mother? Before the police do?'

★ ★ ★

There was an option, on quiet nights, of the long-shift producer or editor getting an hour or two's sleep in a bedroom over the road at the Langham, which was still a BBC building. One of the editors was very keen on this, and would regularly knock back a glass of Night Nurse and a double whisky and fall unconscious until woken at 4 a.m. I tried it myself, catnapping as I had learnt to do on small boats, but always woke up feeling so terrible that it was not worth it. In the end I either stayed in the office through the small hours reading, or got a change of scene by going out for a walk round Oxford Circus in the dank night air and then coming back in for a quick game of Snap or Poker with the commissionaires behind the main reception desk.

In those bleak hours it always seemed quite impossible that anyone could be fit to do two-and-a-half hours of potentially chaotic studio production. But somehow, when the running order was done and a late story had come in from California to be processed, the team would perk up. The presenters rolled in at about 5.30 in those days, far later than now, to be given their cues and have the live interviews

151

explained to them. Then you went into the studio, sat at the desk, wound up your stopwatch, got your notes together and pushed off down the slipway — splash! into the deep water.

And it was fine. Few items on *Today* ran more than four minutes, and there were mechanical network-breaks to be hit, where regions opted out; so even if there were no live guests it was impossible to nod off or lose concentration. The ten-minute news bulletins on the hour provided a brief dangerous respite, but black coffee kept you going. So did the jokes: Timpson had few more appreciative listeners than me for his ho-hos. When the programme ended, we all spilled back into the office and wrenched off the cap of the whisky bottle, using it to wash down leathery Marmite toast or mini-sachets of Alpen. After a somewhat disjointed handover conference with the next shift, I would stagger downstairs to see whether I could still find the entrance to Oxford Circus tube and remember my way back to the silent white haven of Miranda's flat. Sometimes I failed, and woke up at Edgware.

The attachment ended; a few months later the twenty-two-hour experiment ended also. But I cannot regret it. Everyone, at some time in their youth, should spend a period working impossible shifts or sea-watches. It is cheaper than a mind-altering drug or an expedition to the South Pole, and you get over it faster. But you learn much the same lessons about yourself, your limits, and the tricks your mind can play.

10

Oxford Morning

It was good to be back in Oxford, with the green leaves on the trees and the same old colleagues — more or less — whom I had left six months before. The little house in Cutteslowe had lost some of my original flatmates and was gradually becoming a Radio Oxford flophouse. We had a dry, laddish young reporter called Graham with a ginger moustache and an equally ginger cat, Tigger. We also, when autumn came, had a short let of one room to a TV reporter. He was detailed to cover the trial of the Bradford joiner who turned out to be the actual killer of the same Lesley Whittle whose death had haunted my night-shifts. I was fascinated and repelled by the way that TV reporters had to have their hair and shiny noses touched up before they could do a piece to camera, and very glad not to be one of them.

Then a news agency reporter called Roger Clark moved in, and eventually, while our real boss was away, we even added to this motley crew the acting station manager, John Murray, who decided we were the cheapest digs going and that it wasn't worth uprooting his family for a mere three months.

It says a lot for the general camaraderie and lack of oppression on the station that all of us

— boss, lowly station assistant, and two freelances — lived in perfect amity and never brought our disputes home. We used to sit and watch The Brothers of an evening, beer in hand, cackling with glee at the boardroom soap opera and dipping into the same bag of crisps as the manager, even though the next morning one of us might turn up in his office with a heavy-duty grievance or a financial demand. We kept a most effective glass wall round our ramshackle home life, and I doubt very much that Local Radio Directorate in London ever knew a thing about the arrangement.

Indeed, the informal democracy of Radio Oxford was particularly striking to me after working in network radio where hierarchies are clearer. Perhaps the most remarkable example concerned Humphrey's New Jingles. For some reason, perhaps fearing competition from a new commercial station over at Reading, the programme organizer decided that we should have musical 'stings' or sung jingles in the style of Radio 2 (you know, session singers crooning 'Bee-bee-cee — Radiooowww — Two — Jim-meee Younggg!').

Humf, being a man of idiosyncratic taste and also a bit of a tease, resolved to commission ours from the Kings' Singers, the musically immaculate but slightly precious *a capella* group of the day, who came complete with soaring counter-tenor and were generally heard only at Christmas when we played their smash-hit medieval carols. The jingles were, frankly, unspeakable. Try and imagine them, leaning

154

heavily on the effect of a counter-tenor and a set of seriously posh voices. One went:

For the weather and the nyeewwws . . .
And y'r own local vieeewwwssss . . .
Ray-diow Oxforrrrd!

Even worse — so dreadful I almost cannot type it out — was a lilting one which went:

For a cheerful little earful —
Ray-diow Oxforrrrd!

We were given these horrors on cartridge, and ordered to play them at programme junctions. I never did; not even once. Nor to my knowledge did anybody else on the station except Humphrey himself and — from time to time — the accommodating Thomas Prag. We not only disliked them, but had a powerful instinct that our audience, particularly the car workers at Cowley, would be so enraged by them that they would quite rightly rise up and scrag us. Radio 2's equivalent ones were at least neutral soggy muzak. These had such an edge of mortarboard and choirmaster, whimsy and patronage, that we could not bear to use them.

And nobody ever forced us to, and before long the whole ghastly project faded. There are other stations, and other networks, where such horrors are imposed by management regardless of absurdity and staff protest. Not at Radio Oxford. Good luck to it.

Very soon after I got back, it was put to me

that the morning programme, daringly titled *Oxford AM*, needed refreshing, and that my experience on *Today* might be useful. What with the general habit of democracy and the argumentative tendency on the station, an eccentric system was settled upon whereby there were two morning presenters — myself and Tony Adamson, the sports chief — who would present the programme on alternate weeks. In our week off-air, each would act as reporter-producer for the other one, working with the Newsroom to gather material and set up the programme the night before. Towering over both of us would be the new programme editor, Mike Hollingsworth (the same who in the 1990s became a recurrent tabloid headline when he left his wife for Anne Diamond, then left Anne Diamond after the birth of several children, became involved in some fracas involving a female disc jockey, a police station and a punch in the eye, and then set up home with yet another, yet younger girlfriend). At the time Mike was just a very sharp radio producer, fresh from helping to evolve the *Jimmy Young Show* on Radio 2 into a news and current affairs interview programme between the records.

He was very good indeed. The young Mike was ambitious for himself, ambitious for the programme — which ran non-stop from 6 till 9 a.m. — and therefore ambitious for us. He was as different from Andy Wright as night from day, and certainly not as lovable; but he was very, very good, and I learnt much from his craft, his vision of rapid current affairs programming, and

156

his fanatical insistence on getting things right. If he thought a story needed the Chief Executive or the Minister, that was who he insisted on getting. If he thought it should be done live, it would be. If it involved a hook-up with another part of the country, he would nag London Control Room until he got it. If he thought one of us was getting lazy about making features for the other, or sounding dull or sing-song or lacklustre or unfriendly as presenter, then he would tell us. He would not let friendship or general esteem or tact or a desire for a quiet life stand in his way. He threw his weight around. So we did a good programme and got gratifying little scoops.

We even sold some to the network. In my first years at Radio Oxford we ran masses of wonderful stories and tapes which we could have passed on to *Pick of the Week* or *Today*, but somehow the local staff rarely bothered to submit them: our little world was enough, and who cared about feeding material to the big, rich London BBC? But now it was different. I had been up there and survived, and Mike knew he had only left it for a very short while. Our focus was wider. We sent stuff up, and rejoiced when we happened to be breaking a national story.

My own focus was widening, too: I had discovered sailing, took night classes in navigation, and passed the odd empty half-hour of the day sending Morse code flashes across the corridor to the chief engineer, Cliff Wright, who had a Navy background and tested me on my technique. I had also begun writing again, for the first time since university. This was to the credit of Barry Norman, who got so fed up with me complaining about how I 'really wanted to write, but . . . ' that on his way into the *Today* studio one Saturday morning he snarled, 'Stop whingeing then, girl, and bloody well write something.'

So I did squibs for the old *Punch* magazine, about odd pursuits like canal-restoration or miniature hovercraft racing, and they later became my first book, an anthology called *Britain at Play* (I had got over my obsession with recording workplaces). All in all, I got away from Oxford more. In retrospect, I can see that the local radio life couldn't have lasted much longer than it did; yet I was still much in love with the area, and adding daily to a troop of local contacts and friends.

One favourite was George Gibbes, an elderly Russian who was the adopted son of Sydney Gibbes, the Yorkshireborn tutor of the last Tsarevich. They had fallen in together in the Ukraine during the confused period after the tutor left the doomed Imperial family at Ekaterinburg. After Gibbes died, George remained keeper of the memory, and guardian of a moving Russian Orthodox chapel in an Oxford back street. It was full of White Russian relics like Tsar Nicholas' old felt boots, and the little Tsarinas' last copy-books from their lessons in exile. During the long quiet evening on the station, carefully editing the story, I listened to George's unselfconsciously emotional voice as he told the story and felt again the extraordinary power of personality that breathes through recorded speech. It was blind, as radio always is, and George had to describe the relics around him; yet I felt no need to film him or them. The cold eye of the camera would have broken the spell, as far as I was concerned. The incredible link with old, sad history was all there, albeit invisible; it resonated in the sound of his walking heavily round the room, the moments of silence when his hand fell on a revered object, the way the old voice suddenly trembled, then soared with passion and indignation.

I enjoyed the early hours I kept during my week on-air: dawn shifts have always energized me. I relished the loneliness of responsibility, like holding a sea-watch alone, and loved to wake up the Beckley transmitter at 5.45 with first of all a constant tone, then pulse-tone, then finally our signature tune. I liked the early, more musical part of the programme, gently nudging the county into wakefulness; fresh from *Today*, I also enjoyed the way it shaded into a denser news magazine. I liked to keep Radio 4 tuned in to my headphone controls, so that during the longer tapes or records I was playing to Oxfordshire I could keep tabs on my old colleagues and see whether they had stories we ought to lift. I loved a breaking story, with Mike snapping down the telephones in the Ops Room at eight o'clock and barely giving me time to understand it before I started explaining it on the air.

The week off-air as reporter was different, but could be equally interesting. I still liked getting out with a heavy Uher on my shoulder, and bringing home the bacon. However, a degree of friction began to arise between the *Oxford AM* team and the rather staid Newsroom. If we found a story that looked good — whether by news cutting, hearsay, or some arcana like the *University Gazette* — we told the elderly news editor. When he said it was 'not a runner' or that there was 'nobody free to chase it up', we tended to chase it up ourselves, record it, and put it out. Getting wind of this, the Newsroom would not unreasonably demand that we 'give them a line' for the local news bulletin, especially if this otherwise happened to be full of very dull stuff achieved by ringing round the police and fire stations. So we would give them their line, but grudgingly, because it meant that the impression was given that they — brave newshounds — had got the story and we feature-bunnies had merely done a 'package' following it up.

The friction was always there; and when it came to my annual report — a gruesome BBC ritual — the station manager read out to me, among the general flannel, the allegation that 'some colleagues find her difficult to work with'.

I was outraged. I quivered like Lady Bracknell. In my own opinion, I was, and am, a pussycat to work with. An amiable pushover, a team player. So I queried this.

'Which colleagues, John? *Who* finds me difficult?'

'I can't say, it's confidential.'

'Then you can't put it down on my record. I insist on knowing which colleagues. There's only one, isn't there, really? In the Newsroom?'

'I can't say.'

Eventually I insisted on my statutory right to add my own note to the record. I wanted to put 'Only stick-in-the-muds knocking retirement find her difficult to work with', but it was not allowed. Eventually we settled on a form of words. But the seed of my leaving was sown. Much as I still relished life in this little bubble, much as I would miss Tony and Andy and Sally and Tom and Mike and Karen and John and Uncle Tom Cobbleigh and all, I understood that very soon I would have to get off the staff of the BBC and go freelance.

I would have to shake off the unspeakable patronage of the personnel lady and the patriarchal unfairness of the report system. I would have to sell my services cleanly, for what they were worth, and never again be labelled with a BBC civil-service grade (I was, in fact, still only on OP3, like a tyro station assistant, though my pay was made up when I was doing *Oxford AM*). Another small irritant was that although the BBC had in the past paid for driving lessons for several other OP3s, it refused to pay for mine, even though it was made clear that once I passed I would be expected to drive the radio car. As I couldn't afford a car of my own, I would have been buying expensive lessons entirely for their benefit. Given the unpaid overtime I had lavished on this station for three years, I thought that was a bit steep, and it is amazing how these small unnecessary meannesses rankle. Anyway, out of sheer spite I didn't learn, and always had to have Cliff or Derek with

161

me when I took the car out on live reports.

So there was a general sense that it was all cracking up, though without particular bitterness. In the end I served a year on *Oxford AM* before, one ordinary afternoon, I found myself humming 'Come back, Paddy Reilly, to Ballyjamesduff', and sniffing the cold sharp Oxford air and looking out of the plate-glass windows two floors up from the car showroom. Like the Mole in *Wind in the Willows* going 'Drat spring-cleaning!' I muttered 'Drat local radio!' And without thinking any further, I put my head round the door of the new programme organizer, who was Andy Wright, and asked with unedifying flippancy: 'Hey, Andy, do you believe that there is a tide in the affairs of men which, taken at the flood, leads on to fortune?'

'Yup,' he said. 'Probably.' He pushed his headphones more firmly over his ears, adjusted his glasses, and pulled a long strip of tape out of the editing machine in front of him.

'So do you think I ought to resign now, and seek my fortune as a freelance?'

'Why not?'

He had not, I think, heard a word I was saying. But the omens were clear enough, and I went next door and told John Murray, the acting manager, that I was resigning. He responded as managers always do when their pond is ruffled — with a hunted, panicky stare and a cry of, 'Oh, God, what have we done now?'

I persuaded him it was nothing personal, just the tide of fortune, and fixed a departure date. And that was it for my local radio life and my

162

career as a BBC staff member.

Except that it wasn't quite all. Olive Gibbs, Lord Mayor of Oxford and a stalwart friend of the station, decided that after all this time I deserved a send-off. She offered to hold a drinks party in the Mayoral parlour for me and said I could invite a dozen or so people to drink my health before I went. So I had Len Soden the sweep, and Dennis Payne who found me all the war heroes and knew everything there was to know about big bands, and the chap with the herd of pedigree goats, and other cherished interviewees from town and country, and we all said goodbye in style. I loved Olive Gibbs for that gesture. No honour or compliment I have ever had since has meant as much.

11

Errands for Auntie

When I resigned from my job at Oxford I had no guarantee whatsoever of any other work. But that was how it was for the class of 1971; as educated people we had no fear of long-term unemployment because such a thing had hardly been heard of. 'Graduate unemployment' only became a familiar concept later in the 1970s. Our lot were suicidally confident that there would always be something we could do for money. Possibly not much money, and not necessarily anything secure or terribly interesting; but if you looked around there were sure to be jobs on offer.

While I was working out my notice I went first to Mike Chaney, the new editor of the *Today* programme. I notice that in Paul Donovan's authoritative history of the programme he quotes Mike as saying, 'I brought in skilful, witty reporters like Paul Heiney, and Libby, and Ed Boyle, to balance the programme.' This conveys a certain gravitas, as if Mike had furrowed his brow for months and headhunted his reporters with care. In fact, what happened in my case was that I rolled in out of the blue and asked whether he had any spare shifts going, and he peered over his glasses, stroked his huge black beard and said, 'Three a week, Tuesday to Thursday, ten hours variable, twenty-five quid a time. OK?'

Whereon I said, 'Only three shifts?' and he said, 'Count yourself lucky, girl.'

So I went next to BBC Radio London and offered myself there, and they said, 'Mondays and Fridays, on trial, eighteen quid a shift,' and that was it. I have my 1977 diary, preserved in some old box all these years, and the back of it is full of scribbled calculations ('3 × £25 + 2 × 18, rent/rates £117 pcm, bills £22, Tube fares £13, weekends/food/amusements £84, NB put away tax money . . . ') and the calculation that if I walked a lot and avoided the Underground, I could save £82.95 a month in a building society. This made me deliriously rich, by my standards. The NB about the tax money was caused by a gipsy's warning from David Mellor, the *Today* reporter, who instructed me that the chief pitfall of freelancing is the dangerous illusion that you actually own all this money they keep paying you. 'Put away a quarter or a third,' he said. 'Just do it! I didn't . . . '

Very soon the Radio London reporting shifts atrophied and *Today* took up five shifts a week, making me even more affluent by my undemanding, unmarried standards. At weekends I took trains down to the coast, and sailed with anybody who had answered my small-ad in *Yachting Monthly*. Sometimes I would go on a Channel race and get back in a Monday dawn, to yawn up on the milk train with all the other winch-gorillas and shamble sleepily into Broadcasting House, hoping to God that the day editor would not send me out before I had had a quiet kip under the Forward Planning desk.

My only other extravagance was the Royal Opera House amphitheatre, and that could be funded by the odd fifty quid for a *Punch* article. Freelancing, it seemed to me, was just the life. I remember walking down the Strand late one night from Covent Garden — past the lights of good old Bush House as it happens — and thinking, 'I am nobody's vassal! I am not a Human Resource! I am Libby Purves Limited, and only as good as my last tape!' Never again would I have an annual report read out to me by some management figure who couldn't do my job to save his life. Never again would I have a personnel interview, performance review or official assessment.

It was a powerful buzz. In the years since, I have sometimes briefly envied friends in newspapers, BBC and similar staff jobs who get maternity leave and pension entitlements, and whose employers know and sympathize when they are ill or stressed. But I have never really regretted the decision to sell my services ad hoc, rather than my identity. I had observed enough of the BBC to know that it grew cruel very quickly when it tired of its performers, and although I still revered its values and its standards I felt it best to sit loose to this particular bronco, ready to spring lightly aside rather than be bucked off and kicked to death as others so often were.

The work, in Coward's immortal phrase, continued to be 'more fun than fun'. I was back in *Today*, with a few familiar faces around and a slew of new ones, and the programme was riding high. Mike Chaney, the new editor, was a big bluff outspoken bear of a man; a tabloid veteran who was only in his late forties but seemed to come from another era. The legend was that Ian Trethowan had personally recruited him from Fleet Street as founder-editor of *Newsbeat*, Radio 1's pioneering yoof news programme, because Mike had twelve children (three from his previous marriage, four by his wife Fran and another five by her previous marriage). Therefore he was assumed by the BBC mandarins to be 'in touch' with youth culture.

Certainly he wasn't afraid of soundbites, jingles or rudery, and nor did he share the rarefied Corporation attitude to the craft. Recruiting Paul Heiney on the strength of one jokey report on Radio Humberside, he famously brushed aside Paul's protestations of inexperience with the words, 'Pah, there's nothing about journalism that can't be learnt in six working days.' It was generally believed — but never proved — that in his *Newsbeat* days Mike supplemented his BBC salary with night-shifts on the back-bench of the *Sun*. Certainly he used to disappear sometimes during the night when he was on *Today*, borrowing the batteries out of a reporter's tape machine to power his bicycle lamp as he pedalled off, God knows where.

As a boss he was the tops. He led from the front and took no nonsense from politicians of either hue (both main parties were alleging bias on a daily basis). He gave praise where it was due and jovial abuse where it was not. He was stout in defence of his reporters. One of the youngest found out years later that he had caused a very hairy legal battle over a genuine mistake in a report, saying 'murder' for 'manslaughter'. Mike had decided that it was not the reporter's fault, and fought the long battle without ever mentioning it to the culprit. On the other hand he brooked no idleness or timidity from either sex. Being a girl was no reason, in his view, not to be sent out alone across the seedier parts of London at any time of night. He would have felt it insulting to make a distinction. One evening I was two hours off the end of my shift, yawning a little over the *Evening Standard*, and he blustered into the main office and said: 'What're you doing?'

'Just waiting to do St John Stevas [the shadow education minister] about this story about kids attacking their teachers.'

'Who else've you got?'

'The guy who wrote the report, and someone from the teachers' union.'

'What about some kids who beat up their teachers?'

'Well . . . no.'

'So go and get some. One of the Newsroom reporters can do the Stevarse clips.'

'But it's nearly nine o'clock. I mean, fair dos . . . '

It was a winter evening, raw and damp.

'You're a f — ing reporter, I pay you to f — ing report,' he said with great good humour. 'So f — off and find me some kids who beat up their teachers.'

I trudged off into the darkness, heavy tape

machine on my shoulder, and suddenly remembered a South London adventure playground I had visited when it opened. I hurried down there, and sure enough there were some affable roughnecks who managed — between them — to scrape up an anecdote or two about incidents in the classroom, and to offer some salty comments on teachers. I was very ethical, and forebore to do what I had first thought of, which was to offer them a fiver each to tell a better tale.

But Mike was right: the sharp, shrill sound of real kids bragging brought the feature to life and gave added point to the comments of the minister and the union representative. Had there been more time we would have found a teacher who had been a victim; but in current affairs you are always rushing, stumbling to catch up with yourself, and for some reason the report had come in very late in the day. But I had been taught an important lesson about not taking the easy route of booking talking-heads. I had also learnt the equally useful lesson that if you wanted a quiet read of the showbiz pages near the end of your shift, the trick was to settle down where Mike Chaney wouldn't see you. The recording channel, perhaps.

Mike's philosophy was summed up when once, presiding over a farewell drink for another of the day editors, the equally black-bearded and bluff Ted Gorton, he said, 'The thing about Ted is that when you came into the office and saw him in the chair, you knew that the shift would be fun.' Chaney liked fun. Blasts of hilarity would be heard from his office, in between the sound of his orotund dictation of frighteningly robust letters to aggrieved politicians and listeners.

The programme itself was not quite as I had left it a year or so before. John Timpson had temporarily defected to television (which he loathed, and did without distinction). Brian Redhead, a Geordie ex-newspaperman with a frightening demotic fluency and yet another beard, had been recruited to present the programme, but didn't want to come south. So, justifying the manoeuvre as a creative bit of regional democracy, Mike and other executives cooked up the idea of 'Inter-City presentation', in which Nigel Rees held the fort at the London end, while Brian introduced tapes and conducted interviews from the BBC Network Centre in Manchester.

It always sounded terrible: most of the tapes still came either from London reporters or from the regions or abroad, so the fact that Brian was sitting in a padded cell in Manchester was irrelevant. It also meant that a producer had to go up and 'run' him in the morning, a deeply unpopular job. One day I was sent up, having done a producer attachment and being therefore deemed 'trained'. I did absolutely nothing from six-thirty to nine but supervise the putting on of three tapes and watch the studio manager open and shut Brian's microphone. At the end of the programme the London editor, a drawlingly public-school character, rang me.

'Thanks for your hard work,' he said.

'I did bugger-all,' I replied.

'Excellent,' he said. 'Seeing as there's bugger all to do.'

Whatever the illogicality of the presentation, to be a *Today* reporter was a joy. One hour you were closeted with a headlouse expert at the London School of Tropical Medicine, the next shivering with apprehension at the heavy footfall of Shadow Chancellor Denis Healey, who never hesitated to swat aside a stumbling question. Then you might be sent out with your recorder to jostle around Downing Street, uncertain quite where to poke your microphone in the throng of far harder-nosed newsmen; then back to the office and a quiet, intense ten minutes face-to-face with the pale heroism of a Russian dissident's wife. Avital Scharansky was, in those years, implacably doing the rounds on behalf of her imprisoned husband. It is hard to recapture now, on the far side of *glasnost* and the fall of the Berlin Wall, how impossible it seemed to us then that men like Scharansky or women like Irina Ratushinskaya would ever be freed. It was harrowing to talk to those who held a flame for them. But they were right. They won. Things can change. To this day I keep a fragment of the Berlin Wall on my desk because it carries that reassurance.

Then you might be catapulted out of the office again to sit before a hissing gas-fire with Dame Marie Rambert, talking of her life in ballet. At one stage in that interview she seized my hand and said, 'Long fingers. A dancer's hand — take off your shoe!' So I did, and she said, 'A dancer's foot! Why are you not a dancer?' The answer, quite palpably, was because I weighed thirteen stone and had already managed to fall over the strap of my tape recorder while simply walking through the door. All the same I played this bit of the tape back to my colleagues in the office with modest pride, and kept the offcut for several weeks before losing it.

The end of the shift was often spent editing. Producers — as I knew from my six months in the job — often edited completely raw tapes from reporters, but if there was any chance I preferred to commandeer one of the rickety office Ferrographs and some headphones, and sit enwrapt in my interviewees, listening to them again and again, searching for ways to cut a few seconds without losing either sense or atmosphere, or putting them into separate bands so I could insert commentary or other sounds to make a miniature three-and-a-half-minute programme.

When you edit people you have met, you achieve an eerie intimacy. This is a real voice, a thing of breath and blood and feeling, yet you can deconstruct it, running it slow or fast as you clip, noting its idiosyncrasies, taking care not to cut off half-a-breath, kindly removing the odd saliva slurp. It could, I suppose, make you despise humanity (as indeed film editors sometimes come to despise the faces and bodies they work on). But more often — whether with ordinary speakers, politicians or polished spokesman — it engenders a whole new respect. In the end, whoever they are, you cherish them. You have worked so close to their breath, their teeth, their heartbeat, their tremors and resonances, that you are drawn in to empathy.

I remember one old man in particular, talking for a feature about the work of Dame Cicely Saunders and the hospice movement. He had, he told me, only a few weeks left, but he blazed with conviction about the hospice and its spirit. I do not remember his face, or anything else about him, but one phrase is still with me: 'Never fear o' dying, whoever you are . . . never fear o' dying. It's all right.' I can hear it, like a remembered shred of music. Sometimes, when we had a moment like that, one of us would call over the night editor or producer or a friend among the reporters just to share it. There was, after all, always a risk that it would be superseded by fresher news, and never heard outside the office at all.

Before you left, you played your work to the boss of the day, if he or she had time to listen; there were some excellent brains in that office then, picky and easily bored and every bit as demanding as Andy Wright had been. There was skinny, restless, ever-smoking Martin Cox, who later helped found 5 Live; bright-eyed little Colin Adams from Newcastle, with the sharpest ear in the world for woolly scripts and non sequiturs; the exuberantly clever and volubly Irish Anna Carragher, who went on to run the BBC in Northern Ireland; Rona Christie, tall and headgirlish, with a deep vein of old-fashioned kindness; and Sue Bonner, whose dedicated longevity on the programme in the end beat all of us. It was a generation that held to high standards, not least in the avoidance of naffery. You could get away with bits of illustrative music or archive in your feature, but not on the crass intrusive level which became more common in the eighties and nineties, and is only now being refined again. After the editors were satisfied — as far as they ever could be — you went home.

I lived in Maida Vale by now, in a rented Church Commissioners' flat. So focused on work was I that one of my main memories of that flat is waking in the morning early, switching on *Today* and listening, more or less agonized, to see how many of my features or interviews had made it. And this, let me tell you, is the drawback of this otherwise wonderful job.

For it is not enough to meet, and listen, and edit, and enjoy your story. If you can't publish it, as a journalist you suffer the torments of the damned. *Today* was well-funded then, and lordly, and subject to the caprice of the news. It had material enough to throw away good features. If a hotter story came up — even though it could only be covered down a crackly line from Bombay — your hours of research, legwork, and toil with a razor blade would be cavalierly bumped off the running order. Maybe the feature would live another day, but more often it would be superseded by a story on the *World at One* or *PM*, or else covered so heavily in the newspapers that the *Today* team would refuse to run it, however interesting or amusing

174

your tape might be. And if news broke during the programme, it would actually be the best features — the ones promoted to the 8.15 section — which were decimated.

So I lay in bed and listened; sometimes all the way through, hoping to hear some word of my features in the presenters' 'coming up next' menus on the hour and half-hour (even then, an item could be trailed, then dropped). The absence of your brain-child in the early segment, from 6.45 to 7.30, could be a good sign: it might mean it was so good it was being saved for peak time. But if 8 passed, and 8.30, the heart sank. Eventually, at six or seven minutes to 9, you knew that unless your cue began to be read out in the next minute, it was doomed.

Then you began to hope that it was. An even worse terror awaited when your carefully balanced, crafted four-minute feature began to be announced with only two minutes of the programme to go. So they were going to run it — the callous bastards! — butchered and unrecognizable. I had been an overnight producer: I knew how vicious you could get with a razor blade when time was pressing and you knew nothing of the hinterland of a story. So I would begin to pray that they *wouldn't* run it after all . . . and then Brian Redhead in Manchester or Nigel Rees in London began to read out the cue, and I listened, appalled, to the carnage of my day's work.

Still, on a good day a busy reporter might score four or even five hits — on-air interviews and features — and everyone you met would say,

'My, you have been busy.' When you scored nothing for several days running, they would kindly enquire whether you 'still worked on *Today?*' It was all very precarious.

It was, however, noticeable that the older reporters did not care nearly as much. They had lives, wives and children to think about. They could afford to say 'Another day, another dollar'. The younger you were, the more you bled inwardly from wounds to your self-esteem.

After a while, I was made a 'forward planning' reporter in the end office, which meant regular hours; this was a mixed blessing. I tended to wangle myself odd jobs which kept contact with the tense, magical night-time world. During the *Observer* Singlehanded Transatlantic Race in which the circumnavigator Dame Naomi James was competing against her husband Rob James in his trimaran, I cut a deal that she would report by radio-telephone via Portishead every few days, on the laborious old-fashioned system of booked shortwave calls. I was the liaison for this operation, and promised Naomi before she left that I would personally be in the studio to take each call on a direct line, so that she did not have to hang on to a lurching, bucketing chart table while shouting extension numbers to uncomprehending BBC switchboard operators.

Eventually, as the time gap widened, the calls began to come in by night, and I would sit by the phone with my tape, ready to go. The race was being traced by satellite for the first time that year, and whenever she rang, Naomi asked where her husband Rob was. She was far more interested in that than in her own race position; indeed she said often that she only signed on for the Atlantic race to stop herself worrying about him. One night, Rob James' satellite bleep from his fast trimaran did not register, and I had a difficult decision to make. We all knew that the satellite system kept losing boats and finding them again, but do you demoralize a weary, storm-tossed singlehander by telling her that her husband has vanished from the plot? Or do you patronizingly tell a direct lie to a formidably bright, adult, tough woman who is briefly at your mercy?

I had ten minutes to decide, and asked nobody, because nobody in the office was a sailor and I — though in a small way — was. I sat for a while in the warm, still, quiet studio, thinking about the Atlantic, then eventually told her that the whole satellite system had failed to come up that day, and that reports were expected later, when she was off the air. By the next time she rang her husband's bleep had reappeared. By a bitter irony, Dame Naomi eventually did lose Rob to the sea: he drowned in sight of harbour, on Salcombe bar, some years later.

The Future Planning Unit — a cubbyhole at the end of the main *Today* office — held me, the PA Sally Lunn, and Paul Heiney. Sally was an accomplished carpenter, and the two of them spent much time designing a self-steering bracket she was making for the stern of his little boat. Ted Gorton was in charge of the office, and did his bit to scupper any chance of romance between myself and Paul with gobbets of misinformation. He told Paul that I was 'very aristocratic' and a 'typical English Rose, very Sloane Square', and told me that Paul was a playboy with a harem of beautiful women. It took us both months to work out that this was utter fantasy on his part.

In any case, Paul and I began, quite frankly, as rivals. Mike Chaney was very keen on regional coverage, and one of the best jobs around was to 'beat up a region'. You vanished for four or five days, on expenses, and were expected to immerse yourself in the local press, make new contacts for the programme, send in some piquant stories from the field, and return with three or four features about under-reported aspects of life and news in that area. Paul always seemed to manage to be sent to Cornwall, or some other scenic seaside place, while I — still unable to drive — ended up trudging round Oldham or sitting in the office gloomily re-working the obituary of Marshal Tito for the third time (oh, how he lingered).

However, I did once manage to get sent out to the farthest reaches of East Anglia. I spent five glorious days travelling around on local buses and trains, reported on the sodden misery in the aftermath of the Wisbech flooding, and met the Student Cross pilgrims going on foot towards Easter at Walsingham. Travelling remote parts of Britain by public transport has great advantages, as Bill Bryson was to illustrate years later. You pick up all sorts of interesting resonances, some of them dating all the way back to Henry VIII.

178

On the bus to Walsingham, a nice lady in a quilted jacket explained to me in a hushed voice that, 'Protestants and Catholics are Quite Friendly now in the town, but none of us like people who *turn*. Either way.'

On that same trip I covered the Shire Horse Show at Peterborough, a colour piece on which Mike Chaney was most insistent. 'Get there at 4 a.m. and find some little old groom with a face like a walnut, polishing a big horse that snorts a lot,' he instructed me, with that tidy precision which characterizes the tabloid mind. So I did, and fed in the interviews and sounds of the show that same morning from the Peterborough transmitter.

That was a treat in itself for a radio romantic like me: the dawn coming up with scudding pink clouds, the orderly Reithian decency of the transmitter building with its ships' clocks, the pleasure of mixing and feeding my report in live from a ramshackle studio that could not have changed much since the 1930s. As I walked out into the fresh morning, and irresponsibly hitch-hiked into Peterborough because I could not get a taxi, I was perfectly well aware that I had one of the best jobs in the world.

12

A Bit of Trouble

Storm-clouds were gathering in the first months I spent as a *Today* reporter. It turned into the nastiest year in the history of the programme. Ian McIntyre, the new Controller of Radio 4, was a man of fixed and idiosyncratic ideas, and one of them — unfortunately — was plain barking mad. Despite the awkwardness of its two-city presentation the *Today* programme of 1977 was vigorous, cheerful and popular: there was more than enough in the nation and the world to keep it varied and interesting from 6.30 until 9, and in Brian Redhead at last it had the ideal presenter — idiosyncratic, bumptious, original, cheeky, newsaholic.

But the Controller felt that there were too many news magazines on his network, and also expressed a view that the makers of them were too narrow and newspaperish in their attitudes. He had some vague idea of the radio Renaissance Man, and urged producers to have 'outside interests', once famously remarking that he would like to think of them playing the violin or writing poetry as well as obsessively following the news (he plainly had not heard about Jolyon's egg business). He axed *Newsdesk*, the seven o'clock in the evening programme, and the Saturday edition of *Today*. This was not a disaster; one *Today* less was bearable, and what with *The World at One, PM* and *The World Tonight* there was a case for giving the Radio 4 nation a rest from current affairs between 6.30 and 10 p.m. Nor was Ian McIntyre himself quite the madman that we thought him at the time; a long-serving BBC type, he later ran Radio 3 with reasonable success and has written a definitive biography of Lord Reith.

But it must be said that what he did to *Today* was unforgivable. He explained (as far as I could make sense of it) his theory that listeners should come to the news in shorter, more intense bursts, their powers of concentration refreshed by lighter things. So he divided the programme into two parts, one of twenty-five minutes and one of thirty-five. The first began at 7.10 after the news, the second at 8.10. In between, under the care of a separate department, he put a programme — if you could dignify it by that name — called with plonking desperation *Up to the Hour*.

It was terrible. Mike Chaney, with unusual restraint, described it to Paul Donovan in his history of the programme as 'absolute crap, the floor-sweepings'. A typical edition would consist of programme trails for the rest of the day on Radio 4 and some embarrassing little interview with a programme-maker, then Thought for the Day, a piece of irrelevant music, and something coyly described as 'our little treat', which was generally a bit of an old Victor Borge comedy record, or Bob Newhart's 'The Driving Instructor'. Its cardinal sins were tweeness,

181

pointlessness, and above all an utter lack of relevance to the morning, the breezy exciting newstime we had created.

It was desperately demoralizing. We had good material coming out of our ears, a whole world to report on, stories to tell, questions to ask, real jokes and oddities about real life in the real Britain. We hungered and thirsted for our stolen minutes — we had lost a full hour, even if you discount fixed points like weather forecasts. It was a kind of physical pain to hear our lively programme stop dead each day for the 7.35 edition of *Up to the Hour*, with its laborious, miserable fillers and dead old joke records. Even those who made it were pretty unhappy at what they were doing.

Through that awful winter, though, there were acts of heroism. Mike Chaney was outspoken in his criticism of the Controller, although he knew it might cost him his job (it did, in the end). And in a famous act of defiance the announcer Peter Donaldson said it for us all. One morning, opening the network in his beautiful, deep-brown, decorous announcerly tones, he announced himself as 'Donald Peterson' and ran slowly and deliberately through a list of what the other three networks were doing, concluding, 'But if you're listening to Radio 4 — I'm afraid you're stuck with *Up to the Hour*.'

He could have been sacked on the spot for that. He knew it. But the wave of love and gratitude that rolled towards him from all over the great battleship building was unstoppable. We ran towards him in corridors, we wrung his hand and promised to throw ourselves under the Director-General's car and firebomb the executive lavatories if they dared give him the push. Peter couldn't get into a lift without someone grinning and thumbs-upping and (in the case of the more emotional of us) hugging him.

His gesture mattered all the more because he was a Radio 4 announcer and newsreader, the very quintessence of Old BBC gravitas. Announcers on this network are a remarkable breed: at their classic best they are clear, authoritative, not unfriendly but not chummy either. They have the humility to act as human signposts, not drawing attention to themselves or showing off, yet the humanity to indicate by the slightest twitch of their voice that they too have been moved, or amused, or surprised by the programme they are signing off. The greatest announcers — David Dunhill, Bryan Martin, Peter Donaldson, Brian Perkins, Laurie Macmillan, Harriet Cass, Charlotte Green — have always embodied in their unassuming presence the very best of Radio 4 and hence the soul of the BBC. Without undue solemnity or any pomposity, they represent a clear line back to the vision of the Reithian pioneers, providing information, inspiration, education and entertainment. They are trusted, and they know it.

So it mattered intensely that one of these domestic gods, one of the very *Lares et Penates* of the network, had done the unthinkable and declared that McIntyre's rubbishy *Up to the Hour* was a disgrace to Radio 4 and a grief to us all. We loved Peter for it. Some of us still do.

Fortunately, he was saved for the nation and went on to become Chief Announcer, passing on the torch to those who announce the programmes to this day.

The madness passed. Aubrey Singer took over as Managing Director of Radio after many horrible months, and rapidly appointed a new Controller of Radio 4. Ian McIntyre was removed to Radio 3, where he could play Renaissance Man to his heart's desire, *Up to the Hour* was axed, and the *Today* programme returned to its proper length on the Monday after he left. It would be hard to devise a more pointed defeat: Mike Chaney's principled objections had been proved justified, and his arch-enemy had gone.

So the BBC — which forgives a lot, but *never*, *ever* forgives anybody for being in the right — pushed Mike out of his job, replacing him with a big affable chap called Ken Goudie from the Newsroom.

We were as cross about that as we had been about *Up to the Hour* itself. Mike was a patriarch, and a great party man (at one of his parties, Paul Heiney and I finally began the courtship which led to a long and happy marriage). So on his last day we all went out drinking, in one of those eye-watering *Today* gatherings at Efes restaurant which lasted many hours and involved a lot of shouting. Then we took our fallen editor to crew Paul's little boat along the coast from Rye, so that he could not spend the evening brooding on the end of his mainstream news career. The big man fell asleep as soon as we put out to sea, but when the boat fell off a particularly steep wave he stirred.

Half-asleep, bleary-eyed above the bushy beard, he muttered: 'You'll be all right, won't you? You two and all the others? You'll get along with the new chap? You'll be all right?' 'Yes,' we told him. 'Go back to sleep. It's OK. It's just the bloody BBC, right?'

Later, in 1980, a gang of us went up to Norfolk for the press party at his new job, as launch manager of the new BBC Radio Norfolk. Mike's speech to the assembled local press began, 'As you know I've been thrown on the shitheap, but this is as nice a shitheap as any to be thrown on.' Not one of them reported it. I think perhaps they could not believe their ears.

★ ★ ★

Meanwhile, *Today* was undergoing another relaunch. John Timpson was back from television, and glad to be doing the programme again. Brian Redhead had been persuaded to move down from Manchester for three days a week. Nigel Rees had abruptly quit, to go on to far greater fame and fortune as deviser of the *Quote Unquote* show. There was a need for a third presenter, and one or two were tried out. What with leave and negotiations over what day would be worked by whom, a certain amount of chaos reigned, culminating in a situation where poor John Sergeant, then a Newsroom reporter, was asked to do the two-and-a-half-hour programme all on his own.

While this went on I was down at Stonehenge for a couple of days, interviewing aggressive druids who were at odds with the authorities over how close they could get to the stones with their white sheets and made-up pagan chants. I had had a medical feature on the programme that morning, something about retinitis pigmentosa, and to my horror, as I lay awake in my Wiltshire bed-and-breakfast I heard it go out with a disastrous cut in it, made by some sleepy overnight producer. It had become medical nonsense. I knew there would be serious trouble from the eye surgeon I had interviewed, not to mention the Retinitis Pigmentosa Association, etc. So when I got back from the stones to find an urgent message to ring Ken Goudie, I was ready.

'Ken, it was fine leaving me. Someone cut out a sentence. Tell the doctor — '

'What? It's nothing about doctors.'

'Oh. What, then?'

I yawned. It had been an early morning. I thought perhaps there was another West Country story to plod on to, though it would be odd for the programme editor himself to ring about such trivia. I hoped not. I planned to go sailing.

'It's just, will you please present the programme next week with John Sergeant?' said Ken. 'He's not doing it long-term, and he shouldn't have to do it solo. You see how we're fixed. You've done this sort of thing on Radio Oxford, I hear.'

'Oh. Fine.' I packed my scruffy bag and went back to London. When I got into the office Ken

Goudie was there, and Aubrey Singer looming behind him: both were large and impressive men in every dimension. It was like being escorted into harbour by a school of whales.

'Would you,' said Ken, 'do it on a permanent basis?' Clearly, someone else must have resigned, refused, or been sacked while I was on the train. It seemed to me that either they didn't know what they were doing — they hadn't even tried me out — or else they were cynical enough to think that I would be easy to sack if they didn't like the way I sounded.

So I thought for a bit, then said: 'The thing is, Ken, it's a bit like being asked to marry Henry VIII. Very flattering, but risky.' I said I would give it a week, on the clear understanding that if they didn't like it I could have my old reporter's job back. I knew their little ways: various people had been try-out presenters over the time I had known the programme, and when they stopped being presenters they vanished from its ambit. I loved the programme very much — our reborn, full-length, triumphant, post-McIntyre *Today* was still a treasure — and I was not going to risk losing contact with it entirely just because some mandarin was too bloody embarrassed to look me in the eye after sacking me as a presenter.

For very similar reasons I had never asked for a longer-term contract than the loose arrangement whereby I worked week by week. That was Paul's advice. He warned me: 'Don't take a contract. Just keep turning up to work and clocking in. If you've got a contract, after three or six months or whatever it is some committee

187

has to sit down and seriously ask themselves whether they need you. If you haven't got a contract it never comes up for renewal. You're just a running expense, like lunch.'

And so it was that for the first six months of my three-and-a-half years as a *Today* presenter, I was technically casual labour. I only signed a contract when we had all settled down together and got happy; it was, I suppose, like living together before marriage.

There was something else I had to break to them after the first few days, before they did the big press release. This was July and I needed six weeks off in December and January. I had a chance to crew across the Atlantic on a 50-foot ketch called *Makahiki*, and I wasn't going to pass that up for anything (especially given the Henry VIII aspect of the new job). Ken and Aubrey swallowed a bit, and then agreed, on condition that I would pose in Regent's Park peeking through a life-ring for the *Evening Standard*, and let them make a little press story out of it.

The other little story they could have had was one I didn't mention. I had already more or less moved in with Paul, who was still a reporter on the programme. Having a mild horror of personal publicity, we decided to tell nobody. I lied my way cheerfully through several interviews, pretending to have no time for boyfriends ('She has never married,' wrote the *Telegraph* magazine, as if I were sixty). Paul began to look for jobs elsewhere, eventually moving to TV.

Meanwhile I settled down to what would be

my pattern for the next three years: presenting the programme four days a week while the chaps each did three. On Mondays and Tuesdays I partnered John Timpson, that legend from my convent childhood. On Thursdays and Fridays I co-presented with Brian Redhead. On Wednesdays I got the day off, and they had to rub along together somehow. It was not, at that stage, thought politic to make them share a studio more than one day a week. They really didn't like each other much.

13

Up Early, by Land and Sea

I enjoyed my few first days with John Sergeant. He was an affable chap with a dry wit, a familiar figure among the Newsroom reporters and correspondents who drifted in and out of the *Today* office. I had worked with him as a trainee producer a year or so before, and he was one of the easiest to get on with. During the tapes we muttered a bit about the loopy behaviour of the department, hurling presenters to and fro like confetti; and we helped one another limp through the technical business.

This was considerable: you had to hit fixed points like the 7.55 weather forecast and the Greenwich Time Signal, remember to read out the short weather at 29 minutes past each hour, to give timechecks, get the Thought for the Day bishop's name right and glare at him if he looked like overrunning, all with an intermittent squawking from the producer in your head-phones. Sometimes you had to save a few seconds by cutting your cue even while you read it, sometimes you were abruptly told to pad out an empty patch with a curiosity from the papers or a quick crack. You had to think swiftly of a way to change the mood if the producer gave you an impossible transition between frivolity and deathly seriousness. Producers — as I knew from being one — had a tendency to get so obsessed with timings and network-breaks that they would fail to notice they were juxtaposing a story about a dog that juggles sausages with one about the failure of crops in a famine zone.

Although as presenter you are not quite as important as you think you are, there is a genuine minor skill involved in keeping a complex programme sounding relaxed, a thin one sounding interesting, and the whole machine rolling smoothly along. It is a bit like being a juggler in the kind of novelty act where audience members hurl unpredictable objects at you — a ball, a banana, a pencil, a paperback — and you adapt to keep them all flowing evenly through the air.

I found that anchoring a live news programme in this agile medium is very different from the art of reporting. It is fussier, more constrained, as much about living on your wits as about preparation beforehand. Also, you have to offer more of yourself than a reporter does. Although showing off is noxious, a presenter needs to yield up at least a little bit of knowable personality. It was plain that John Sergeant didn't really like it all that much. A born star reporter, and a considerable comic when fully relaxed, he has always been happier either clowning around for pure fun — as on *Have I Got News for You* — or else out at the sharp end of a breaking story, acutely focused, speaking as one who knows. Everybody's favourite image of John is the moment during Mrs Thatcher's downfall when she emerged from the building in the background and crept towards him undetected while he was doing a live report into the news, so the London presenter had to squeak, 'She's behind you, John!' as if it was a panto. Wonderful things like that don't happen to a chap in studios. There are security doors to prevent rogue Prime Ministers creeping up behind you.

Certainly in summer 1978 John was definitely not ready to be tied down to a studio chair. He left at the end of his week with an audible sigh of relief.

I, on the other hand, rather enjoyed it. On a dull morning, with lots of tapes and nothing very new breaking anywhere in the reportable world, it could be a considerable effort to stay cheerful and equable as you went through the motions. But then, there were few dull mornings. Mike Chaney had gone into exile in Norfolk, but his old team was largely intact and his spirit prevailed. To keep myself sharp I even managed to have the occasional editorial dust-up with my favourite sparring-partner, another ex-newspaper-man from Essex known universally as Badger. He and I had first crossed swords when Louise Brown — the world's first test-tube baby — was born, and I recorded an extraordinary interview with the Scottish Cardinal Gray. He explained that according to Catholic doctrine as seen by him, IVF was wrong — not for any deeply philosophical reason concerned with meddling with the building-blocks of life, but because of 'the sinful means used to produce the male sperm'. The sin of Onan: spilling your seed upon the ground.

Badger absolutely refused to put this interview on the air, on grounds of taste and (I suppose) apparent battiness. I took a more adventurous line and priggishly informed him that he had no right to censor a valid point of view put forward by a qualified Cardinal with a red hat. He won. He was the boss.

Not long into my new life, the same subject came up again. We presenters had to rewrite tape cues in our own words: one morning I wrote one about a new fertility technique. Having listened to the tape and read the notes, I said in the cue that it 'brought hope to women who are infertile because of problems with their fallopian tubes'. I thought it was important to be clear, since it was medical. I also thought it important not to suggest to desperate women that this new method was relevant to *all* forms of infertility.

Badger, part of whose job was to look over the cues, gave it back to me with the last seven words heavily crossed out. I refused to read it out that way, on the grounds that it gave an erroneous hope to a far-too-wide constituency of infertile women. Badger, with classic tabloid primness, snarled: 'Look — people *just* don't want to 'ear stuff about women's *choobs*, first fing in the morning.'

So I refused to read it out at all, and gave it to John Timpson, who raised his eyebrows at me and went 'Hah!' and insouciantly read it Badger's way. John had been brought up as a downtrodden cub reporter on the *Dereham and Fakenham Times*, and knew the pointlessness of arguing with editors. Following this incident, four of the women producers and editors on the programme joined with me in an informal, secret but dedicated alliance called the Fallopian Five. Our aim was to infiltrate gynaecological words on to the programme without Badger noticing. The eventual winner would be anyone who manoeuvred Timpson into the position of having to say 'uterus'. Or 'cervix'.

How dated it all seems now! Only a few years later, the first AIDS panic swept over the nation and suddenly it seemed as if every BBC presenter was talking, in earnest tones, about little else but embarrassing bodily fluids and tubes. Victor Lewis-Smith, then a rather wonderfully troublesome talks producer, expounded the theory that our AIDS propaganda had nothing to do with health concerns at all, but that ever since Lord Reith the Corporation had been full of repressed people whose secret, desperate ambition was to name body fluids in public. They had at last found their chance.

★ ★ ★

The hours were curious, but short (how sorry can you be for someone who works a five-hour day?). A car would pick me up at 4.30, and I would flop down in the studio with a polystyrene cup of coffee and skim through the papers, then look at the running order and see which stories I had to introduce or do interviews about. Aware of my comparative inexperience in news, I was obsessively keen to know as much as I could about the items: I listened all through to the tapes that were ready, read background, quizzed the producers, and thumbed through the Atlas to make sure I knew exactly where Nicaragua or Lesotho or Tallinn was on the map, where borders were, what the terrain was like, and so forth.

I learnt the curious art of interviewing a correspondent down a crackling line: it is a stagey business, different from the more challenging and unpredictable business of questioning someone actually involved in the story. When you do a correspondent, you have more or less agreed the questions; in a less chat-obsessed world, after all, the poor man or woman would be allowed just to deliver a straight report. The illusion of conversation with the studio presenter is only there to add informal immediacy. If there is no time to speak beforehand, you leave the questions as open as possible.

What you try not to do is to ask a question they can't possibly answer. Correspondents really, really hate this (Brian Redhead used to do it a lot). The other thing you don't do is to use your question to give the whole answer (cribbed off their news bulletin report half an hour earlier) so that they have nothing to say but 'You're quite right, Brian'.

We had some hot stories to break and to examine in that autumn of 1978. Pope Paul VI died suddenly in early-August, and Cardinal Luciani became Pope three weeks later, only to die a month afterwards, being found at 5.30 in the morning. It precipitated a surreal moment for us when the sportsnews presenter came in looking a bit white and said, in the seconds before we went live: 'Pope's dead.'

'Oh catch up!' John Timpson said, riffling his notes. 'That was a month ago.'

'Nope. He's dead again. The new one, I mean.'

And so we were into a maelstrom of revised running-orders, lines to Vatican City and the inevitable interview with Norman St John Stevas, 'Britain's leading Catholic', which John did while I barracked furiously, arguing that for one thing I was the only cradle-Catholic on the premises and ought to be doing the interview, and that for another it was offensive to assume that just because someone had been a minister in secular government he was any kind of 'leading Catholic'. Nobody listened. *Today* producers tend to have had an awful lot of practice at ignoring complaints from presenters.

Meanwhile the former Liberal Leader Jeremy Thorpe was on trial for murder, the Bulgarian defector Georgi Markov was murdered with a poisoned umbrella, the Shah's rule in Iran began to collapse (we were forever phoning the Ayatollah in Paris), a bakery strike caused panic buying of bread, the *Times* and *Sunday Times* ceased publication because of a strike, and the Jonestown mass suicide shocked the world. In economic policy ministers talked earnestly of the 'snake' of European currencies and the 'five per cent solution'. Mrs Thatcher was rallying the opposition into a formidable force to challenge Callaghan's Labour government, and over in

China (this was to matter to me a great deal later on) a significant thing happened: the *People's Daily* denounced the *Little Red Book of Chairman Mao*. Things were unravelling there, too.

All the same, I jumped ship after only a couple of months. I held to my demand to have December and the first half of January off, and joined a 50-foot steel ketch called *Makahiki*, sailing the Atlantic from the Canaries to Barbados. It simply seemed too good a chance to miss. I don't know what my colleagues thought of this manoeuvre: here we were, with a reborn and reinvigorated full-length *Today* programme, and I was lucky enough to be one of the cherries on top. The winter of discontent was looming, with every kind of political excitement at home and abroad, yet I walked out of the prime job in current affairs for nearly two months. I must have been too busy packing to notice that they thought I was nuts. But I was still young enough, and enough of a 'sixties child, to think that getting a life was more important than getting a career established. Anyhow, having spent the last few days of November presenting the programme live from Edinburgh (I have no idea why, but that is what my diary says I did), I flew to Las Palmas at the turn of the month and joined my little ship.

In the event, it provided a useful mental break. Out on the Atlantic, steering long watches by day and night under the trade-wind clouds and surfing down the occasional gale, cut off from all but short-wave communication for 3000 slow, heaving miles, I had plenty of opportunities to think about what I did: especially about radio, and the fragile dependence we have on voices in the air.

At first I was delighted to be clear of it: 'Heigh-ho for the hols,' as Molesworth said in *Down With Skool*. It is hard work keeping up with all the world's news all the time, just in case you might be asked to do a sudden live interview about Nicaragua at a minute's notice. The first inkling that I might actually *miss* the news came on the dockside at Puerto Rico, Gran Canaria. A beetroot-burnt, open-sandalled pair of feet stopped at eye level as I sat on deck working rope, and their owner (drawn by our British flag) said: 'Football's all off, then. Rain and hail and snow. Trains in trouble too.'

I stared up at him against the merciless sunlight, and suddenly what had up till now been my job, my chore, my daily glut of newsprint and radio babble, changed its aspect to become a more durable and eternally desirable commodity: News from Home. On Greenland's icy mountain and India's coral strand, exiles inevitably care. I knew this from Bush House, and from my father's earnest scanning of the newspapers during my peripatetic diplobrat childhood, but at that moment it entered my heart. Back home, far away in the rainy island, the football's off. What else? Stands Whitehall where it did? Has Thatcher chosen St John Stevas for the Shadow Cabinet? Is my team ploughing? When we reached Tenerife outward bound, I spent a small king's ransom on a two-day old *Sun*, and treasured every word.

★ ★ ★

At sea for the next three weeks, we were at the mercy of the atmospheric layer-cake off which they bounce BBC World Service. In home waters I had often experienced the curious comfort which radio brings to tossing yachtsmen: the inanities of Jimmy Young sounding tinny and reassuring in a yowling Channel headwind, the pock-pock of Wimbledon commentary when the waves are breaking over your pitching bow, the comfort of listening to a slow dramatization of *The Barretts of Wimpole Street* in a dark and insecure Saturday-night anchorage. I had once been sick in a bucket while listening to a Reith Lecture, and night after night in the wild Western Approaches had heard 'Sailing By' before the late shipping forecast and been grateful for the invisible hand of the studio manager — perhaps a friend from my own course — who put it on the turntable.

This comfort, and this surreal inappropriateness, is multiplied a hundredfold on an Atlantic crossing. There was no onboard e-mail or satellite telephony in 1978: apart from the skipper's endless fiddling with his ham radio ('Hello? Sydney? Golf Papa Delta Romeo . . . '). BBC World Service was all we had, and it was tantalizingly intermittent. With a crew of four, working three watches, each of us was often all alone on deck with the rest sleeping. One pouring moonlit night, 250 miles south-west of the Canaries, I caught through the static an edition of *Outlook*. John Tidmarsh, a familiar voice, told me that the US had put a probe on Venus; that the National Maritime Museum had a new gallery; and that I must join the world in mourning Golda Meir. Again, becalmed one night, with no point even trying to steer, I slipped below for a few moments to escape the sight of the mast scything aimlessly to and fro across the moon and heard of a shooting in South London and the Circus World Championships. It all filled that yawning appetite for News from Home — and, curiously, home didn't have to be Britain: Iran, or Connecticut, or Calcutta would do, as long as it was solid ground and not salt water. The world was Home.

In this raw, receptive listening state, I marked and digested several lessons which I resolved to bring back to the business side of the microphone if ever we safely reached land. The first one came after a frustrating hour's attempt to get a sight on the Pole Star while being rolled about like a beanbag. On the radio, suddenly clear, a *News About Britain* reader was sounding (I thought) very smug as he overworked such phrases as 'Our local government correspondent confirms' . . . 'Our home affairs correspondent explains . . . ' and I found myself banging down the *Nautical Almanac* and snarling aloud: 'OK, clever-drawers, since you're so bleeding brilliant, what's our latitude, then?'

Recovering, I acknowledged an eerie kinship

with all those embittered listeners whose letters to *Today* began, 'It is clear that that vicious little chit, Libby Purves, has never brought up a family of twelve and an elderly relative on a fixed income ... ' as if that were a blameable deficiency in myself. The lesson I learnt was that we allow radio voices very intimately into our lives, and that this is a perilous intimacy, because we may eventually come to blame them for not knowing that our cat is unwell when they joke heartlessly about mange, or not making allowances for the fact that we've got the mixer on and can't hear their funny asides.

Even as I cursed that innocent announcer in the corner of the chart table, I knew that I would in turn be cursed, morning after morning, for being a smug nattering dwarf in the plastic box beside the marmalade. And so I have been, and I accept it, and if ever I have annoyed you I am sorry.

The other lesson was not a question of manner, but of content. I had always laughed at the kind of angry correspondent who rages about the removal of cricket scores from the news, but I got my comeuppance with that report on the Circus World Championships at Clapham. I loved that event; after my circus encounters in Oxfordshire I knew a lot of the names. I did not want the jolly, sawdust-romance, isn't-it-awfully-frightening-on-that-trapeze interview which I was offered. I wanted the *results*. Did the Flying Terrells pull off the quadruple somersault? Was Manfred Duval still the high-wire stiltwalking champion of the world?

Nobody told me. Bastards! I vowed never again, if I could help it, to leave a story half-finished. Or, given the unreliability of the atmospherics once we got halfway across, to assume that my listener already knew the basics. No more *Today* cues beginning 'After the week's stirring events in east Liberia' or 'The lesson of Whangarei had many bitter parallels for the torn province of Murmansk . . . ' I would tell them everything, or nothing.

I loved World Service, though; when I was tired and a little afraid and the navigation was uncertain, to hear dear old 'Imperial Echoes' and 'Lilliburlero' was an immense comfort. Big old Bush House was still there, still lit all round the clock and round the year, still sending out News from Home to wanderers. I am sick to my heart, now, at the news that Auntie is gradually giving up on short-wave because more people listen on the Internet. How can they, in the illimitable phoneless wastes of sea or jungle, desert or scrub? How can they if they are poor, or their phone is cut off? How can we have this gift, the free mysterious movement of radio waves, and not use it to the fullest?

Coverage became better as we approached the Caribbean. Just before Christmas, as I was leaning on the wheel watching Venus rise, a scruffy head poked out of the hatch to say cheerfully: 'Your Beeb's in trouble, then!'

Behind him, the skipper pointed out into the darkness and said: 'Dolphin just swam past, asking for you. Had a strike notice in his beak.'

It was a union dispute, a bad one, which blanked the screens for several days. All next day, a mid-Atlantic scab still standing my watches, I strained through the static shusshing to hear some hard news. At dusk the Brazilian mutterings and electric crackle parted briefly to let through some words about 'ACAS . . . normal working resumed . . . Trethowan . . . ' So I wasn't on strike after all.

Then it was Christmas, and by joyful serendipity I was alone on deck for the Queen's Broadcast on a breezy sunny blue day, and it was the year when she interposed her own words with those of her father, George VI, in the 1939 broadcast when he quoted a poem by the otherwise forgotten Minnie Louise Haskins:

I said to the man who stood at the Gate of the Year, 'Give me light that I may tread safely into the unknown.' And he replied, 'Go out into the darkness, and put your hand into the Hand of God. That shall be to you better than light, and safer than a known way.'

Imagine the impact of that, after three weeks out in the darkness and emptiness, groping with the sextant for a known way. The old King's voice, remembered with dispassionate calm by his Queen daughter, crackled off the short-wave radio and crept, as only radio voices can, straight into the very seat of emotion. I gulped. Britain's royalty, at the heart of its great incongruous Commonwealth, has always understood the power of radio. In the first ever

Christmas broadcast from Buckingham Palace George V echoed Reith's vision of radio as a power to overcome isolation:

To men and women so cut off by the snows, the desert or the sea, that only voices out of the air can reach them; to those cut off from fuller life by blindness, sickness or infirmity . . . to all, to each, I wish a Happy Christmas.

Radio speaks to all and yet to each. That is the nobility of it.

And radio brought us safe to land. One day, fiddling with the RDF (Radio Direction Finding) equipment, we picked up not the bleeps of a coastal beacon that we were searching for, but the bop and brass of CBC Radio Barbados. 'This is *The World at One* — brought to you courtesy of Everybody's Stores on Swan Street.'

Way to go, man! It was a frivolous sound after the mystery and austerity of BBC World Service. It might not have that dignity which comes of talking to sea and land and air and ice and jungle and volcano, to all and to each, but its warm local beat was alive with the promise of fresh fruit and fresh water, bars and beaches. As New Year approached and 'Auld Lang Syne' swung to a steel reggae beat, we used the radio receiver to home in on the island, navigating in by the 'null' as if it were an RDF beacon back home. We never bothered with the sextant again.

A couple of days later I was leaning on the bar

in the Bridgetown Sailing Club, chatting up a barefoot man in flowered shorts with a gleaming bare black chest.

'What d'you do?' I asked.

'I'm the Minister of Education.'

He was, too. And a good one, by all accounts. When I told him about navigating in by Radio Barbados he was thrilled, and insisted on whipping me up to the evening show on local TV to tell the story. 'We never get the yachties on, it's a shame.' I told the story, with the pleasing result that for the next week or so everywhere I went people said, 'Hey, lady from the television!' and plied me with Banks' Barbados Beer. Expelled from the boat, my fellow-crew and I had quite a lot of time to hitch round the island while we waited for standby flights.

But the news angel was still hovering, waiting to snatch me back. The item just before me on Barbados TV was an interview recorded earlier in the day with James Callaghan, the Prime Minister, who was at the four-power summit in Guadeloupe. Shortly afterwards he returned to London, tanned and dismissive of the strikes, to the killer headline CRISIS? WHAT CRISIS? It was the beginning of the end of his government, and brought an end to the pendulum years of alternating Tory and Labour regimes in Britain. Five months later, Mrs Thatcher was out there in her pearl earrings quoting St Francis of Assisi and preparing to kick the country into a whole new gear.

So Jim Callaghan and I flew back to Britain.

He was in first class, on his way to be rubbished by the media pack; and I was in ragged jeans in an economy standby seat, on my way home to rejoin it.

14

John and Brian

From 1981 until John's retirement in 1986, the duet of Brian Redhead and John Timpson was a broadcasting legend. They eclipsed the earlier combinations of Timpson-and-de-Manio and Timpson-and-Robinson, because the programme by then had a higher profile in the newspapers, and a political edge which got it into constant disputes with the government.

The two men balanced one another's politics and personality, and grew into what one focus group member in BBC research called a 'perfect and unbeatable duo'. The peculiar chemistry between them, during those five years, helped to keep the *Today* programme high in general esteem through the dangerous period when breakfast television was launched. Even though Redhead and John Humphrys went on to be a more formidably journalistic duo when Timpson left, it is Redhead-and-Timpson that people remember to this day. Like Morecambe and Wise, Abbott and Costello, Marks & Spencer, they became a valuable brand.

So it is a little odd to reflect that for three and a half years before that era truly began, I was the buffer between them. From 1978 to 1981 I was the woman who kept Abbott from Costello, Morecambe from Wise. The routine was that on

Mondays and Tuesdays I co-presented with John, on Thursdays and Fridays with Brian. They only came together for one day a week — Wednesday.

Frankly, neither looked forward to it, and I had the chance of hearing each of them muttering complaints against the other. I did not have trouble with either, possibly because when they were sitting alongside a woman twenty years their junior, they could each feel supreme: head boy, big hitter. If you put them together, they became competitors. So mine was, in retrospect, a peculiar and piquant situation. At the time it was just my job, and I learnt different things from each of them.

I used to get in around a quarter past four. If it was Monday or Tuesday, John would turn up about twenty minutes after me and bury himself in the papers; he was never very sunny until we got on the air. At the other end of the week it was Brian Redhead who breezed into the office as early as I did, fresh from his Barbican flat. He would bustle in, humming and rubbing his hands with glee. Sometimes we sang a chorus or two of 'Keep your feet still, Geordie hinny, let's be happy through the neet' to gee ourselves up, then fell on the material before us and got to work.

Both men were intensely conscious of being more important than me, and got very suspicious if I had more stories to introduce, or better placed ones, or above all more 'lives'. Live interviews were less common then than they are now, when it can sometimes feel as if the whole programme is a sequence of assertive middle-class talking heads. Because live interviews were rarer, all three of us loved the buzz of doing them. On Wednesdays, when the two titans met, the production team had to be as careful about even-handedness as parents of squabbling six-year-olds. In a remarkably candid interview with Paul Donovan once, John said of Brian: 'I could never take politics seriously at all, but to keep the thing balanced I insisted on doing as many political interviews as he did, although most of the time I wasn't too clear what I was talking about.'

I have to admit that the pecking order did not bother me very much. I knew they were older than me, accepted that Brian knew more about politics and politicians, and understood that both of them inevitably had longer memories and therefore ought to have more perspective on current affairs. I also knew that I was a quick learner, and had the advantage of being perfectly at home on the air because of my years on local radio. Once you have had to stagger your way through a whole hour with no material except Canadian Talent Library remixes of 'Che Sera Sera' and scratchy Strauss waltzes, a properly produced and prepared network programme will always feel like a wild luxury.

So I knew that on the air I could hold my own with any harrumphing male, writing cues as good as any of theirs and delivering them with a modicum of dash. Besides, being a bit of a pioneer — nobody of twenty-eight had ever presented *Today* before, and no woman had

209

done it regularly — I did not feel that I had to battle for honours with a couple of middle-aged men. So I was junior — so what? I was there. And after I got back from the Atlantic, in January, the very idea of jockeying for position or being nervous about status became absurd. Whatever happened, none of us was going to drown, so who cared? I liked the job, had a happy relationship going, and owned a half-share with Paul in a 26-foot boat. Life was too good to care whether two old blokes got more goes at interviewing the Director-General of the CBI than I did.

Besides, I was never sure that I would be there for long. Monica Sims, the Controller of Radio 4, was dead set against me. I knew this from successive Programme Review Board minutes in which she went on record as wanting me returned to my 'strong suit', reporting. She felt I was too young and chirpy for the gravitas of the presenter job. Only the backing of Aubrey Singer, the Head of Radio, and the Director-General, Ian Trethowan, kept me in place. Had I been personally insecure at the time, I might have been upset by all this. As it was, I took my fun where I could find it.

'Your trouble, young lady,' Timpson used to growl at me, 'is that your career has just *peaked* twenty years too early.' Maybe he was right.

In truth, I liked my partners. Though both were faultlessly articulate, they were enchantingly different in tone. John Timpson was a small-c conservative from Chorleywood with a grown-up family and a talent for old-fashioned, rather courtly whimsy: *ha-ha, ho-ho, hurrumph-hurrumph*. His instinct was towards mild (and not very sincerely meant) self-deprecation, and gentlemanly behaviour. He would have liked to open doors for ladies, had it not been that the *Today* production team was full of fast-moving, assertive, excitable, commanding ladies like Anna Carragher and Rona Christie, who were through any door and back again with an armful of tapes, scolding all the way, before John could get at the handle.

His grumpiness in the mornings was as well-known as Brian's chirpiness. Anyone getting much more than 'Hrrrumph' out of John before six o'clock was lucky. Some of the more impatient producers quite disliked his famous 'ho-hos': bits of the Peterborough column and jokey cuttings along the lines of CRASH COURSE FOR LEARNER DRIVER, which he delivered with consummate skill. But even they knew perfectly well that a Timpson joke was more than welcome to the morning listener. John's favourite letter was from a woman who had been in a traffic-jam when he read something out, and had looked around to see the drivers either side of her laughing as well.

But he was sometimes very, very funny off the air too, and at the expense of all that he himself seemed to be: middle England, a paid-up member of the lawn-mowing classes. Once, I pointed out how much his neighbours would be pleased about some story in the papers about rising property prices in Chorleywood. 'Oh, yes,' he said. 'They'll be dancing in the streets

211

tonight. It'll be the veleta, mind you, but they'll be dancing.' The delivery was faultless; and because it was a joke just for me (during some tape) he was able to slide an eye sideways and see that it had worked, and that I was giggling, and his grumpiness melted into genuine, showman's appreciation of a good audience.

To understand John properly, you had to know where he came from. It was in the early 1950s, when local newspapers sent their copy to the print works by bus, that John started work as a green reporter on the *Dereham and Fakenham Times*. He polished his pants on the hard reporters' benches in the courtroom and rural district council, did tidy shorthand, and got the knack of keeping on the right side of the gentry (reporters were sent round to the tradesmen's entrance in those days). His modest cottage had a bucket lavatory, collected by the night-soil lorry; he covered amateur dramatics, parochial scandals, Stan the Human Fireball and the darts club annual dinner. Years later, after retirement, he wrote an endearing and enjoyable novel about those days — it is now more or less forgotten, but it should have made him the James Herriot of Norfolk. *Paper Trail* featured a news editor called Mr Juby who was against wounding, cleverdick journalism because you don't hurt people 'on parpus, just to show how hully clever you are'. It also featured a TV director, an alarming New Woman called Cynthia who wears mannish clothes and rides roughshod over her team. Enough said.

In that time John Timpson had learned his

212

values: a kindly, droll, instinctive conservatism, a respect for royalty and the establishment, an affable ruralism to which, in retirement, he has gratefully returned. If you wanted to jolly him out of a particularly grumpy mood in the programme, you had only to mention North Elmham or Fakenham or Weasenham St Peter and his eyes softened. Luckily, I was brought up in rural Suffolk for a few years so I knew the terrain. John had, of course, escaped: he got sick of covering darts club dinners and joined the BBC, working up to be royal correspondent and following the Queen on royal tours. And then came *Today* where he found a use for his nature and his talents, cheering up a nation which was still innately (and like him, with a small c) conservative. Nothing — famine, disaster, the assassination of Earl Mountbatten — seemed too bad when Timpson reported it. That was his strength, and also his weakness.

* * *

Brian Redhead was altogether different. He was the city where Timpson was the grassy suburbs; he was north, John was south; he spoke for the clever, chippy classes who rise through education and let you know it, while John represented the comfortable but unacademic middle-class kid who takes life more lightly, and wears what learning he has with whimsical self-deprecation. John wanted it to be 1950, Brian was more than ready for the New Britain of the twenty-first century (though he died before seeing its birth).

213

Brian had nearly become northern editor of the *Guardian*, and used to announce with tedious regularity, 'I am the only journalist on this programme.' That did not go down at all well with the producers. There was always a newspaper editor inside him, writing — or rather speaking — cutting leaderish opinions which were to get him and the programme into increasing trouble as the Thatcher years progressed. John would never have wanted to edit a newspaper: too much fag. Nor did he want to express his political opinions, because they were his own business.

Brian was verbally acute, mannered, and bumptious. He adored the networking, the party conferences, 'dropping a word in the Prime Minister's ear' of a morning, the sense of being on the inside track. John didn't give a damn about the inside track, and would much rather spend his spare time on his own lawn with a drink. Brian dropped names quite shamelessly. There was a famous occasion when he was in Rhodesia and a row had blown up over sanctions-busting, and he came on and said on the programme: 'Yes, I told Peter Carrington [the Foreign Secretary] and he was as shocked as I was.' The great apocryphal Brianism was, 'I was speaking to a lady the other day — it was the Queen actually . . . ' Whatever you mentioned, Brian already knew about it. I used to get evil satisfaction out of tripping him up — off the air, obviously — on subjects he knew nothing much about and I did, like the sea. But to be fair, he took it well.

He thought himself a better writer and presenter than anyone alive, and though he enjoyed his own flow of words, one of his mannerisms was sometimes to pare down a cue to as few words as possible: short, striking tabloid sentences which actually had a tendency to woeful oversimplification. He told me often that the ideal tape cue, to him, would be one word: 'Hark!' On the other hand, he often pulled a dirty trick on politicians who came in for interview. There would be the Chancellor of the Exchequer (Geoffrey Howe by that time) sitting in the hospitality room next to the studio, and Brian would breeze out and say 'What's this all about then, Geoffrey, I don't understand it at all' and the Chancellor would say 'Erm, it's all a matter of controlling the M3 money supply'.

Three minutes later, back in the studio and live on the air, Brian would begin by saying: 'Chancellor, surely at this juncture the M3 money supply is what you should be controlling?' So the poor devil's first answer would be, 'Er, you're quite right, Brian.'

But he genuinely was brilliant, a born live broadcaster, and beyond his bumptiousness lay a reservoir of high-spirited good humour. He also — not a lot of people know this — had moments of humility. Brian Redhead was nowhere near as arrogant as he was sometimes painted. One small example: his natural glee, his gusto, sometimes betrayed him into sounding joyful when some great catastrophe had happened. That glee was what all of us in the studio felt: the simple vigorous childish pleasure of being first up in the morning with a damn' good story to tell (remember, as a child, running round the house telling everyone 'It's snowing!'? Well, that's what being a *Today* presenter is like). But sometimes Brian sounded atrociously pleased when he shouldn't have; I remember on the morning of the Penzance sleeper crash, hissing at him during a brief twenty-second tape, 'Brian! For f — 's sake, people are *dead*!'

He turned his concerned, comic-bearded face to me and said, 'You're quite right. Thank you,' and toned it down thereafter. He also gave me credit, paternally but with genuine kindness, when I did a good interview or wrote a funny cue. Sometimes we had to swap cues in a hurry, and if he ended up with a good joke or a sharp line which was really mine, he would always acknowledge it to me afterwards with a shrug, saying, 'That was your line, good one too.'

It was later, between his son's death and his own tragically early death, that Brian Redhead developed a strong interest in Christianity, became gentler in his private manner, and even thought of becoming a priest. But although by that time I was watching from afar, I was never very surprised. In spite of all the networking, all the bumptiousness, a man as passionately interested in life as Brian was would inevitably, it seems to me, develop a curiosity about its spiritual wellsprings.

★ ★ ★

Nor was I really surprised that after I left, he and John Timpson grew together. I knew the dynamic. When you sit alongside somebody week after week, in a changing, exciting situation, you inevitably become interdependent. One of you might be doing a live interview while the other is being briefed down headphones for something completely new — a coup, a fire, an unexpected interview with the Soviet Ambassador. Then when he starts, it might transpire that the whole running order has changed and that you must not only shuffle your own cues round but reach across, under your partner's hands, and pull his away to re-order them. Or you might see an awful mis-typing in one of his cues coming up (the most common was 'now' for 'not' and vice versa, which could play hell with your explanation of a government initiative which was either now, or not, happening).

So you would reach over and correct it, without even thinking. In that way we variously saved one another from announcing items about 'The Zimbabwean Patriotic Frump (front)' and reading out telexed weather forecasts announcing 'A wee start to the day with randy spells developing'.

Or again, if ten seconds into his live interview the line went kaput, you would be ready to hop in with the next cue, or hand him one; and he would do the same for you. Or perhaps something dreadfully disruptive would happen, like the sportsnews man getting his foot jammed in the waste-paper basket, and you would be able to laugh together about it on air; unless the previous story had been so tragic that neither of you must laugh at all, in which case you would help one another not to.

Together you would get out of the muddle, whatever it was. Brian once lost his voice very suddenly, and pushed the material across to me to finish his sentence. John once or twice gave me one of his cherished newspaper 'funnies' because I had to pad out thirty seconds when the weather centre line vanished. And so forth. You grow together: it just happens.

From time to time, down the decades, press stories surface about ill humour and rivalry between *Today* presenters, bolstered by some remark made in exasperation at a party (*Today* presenters, being short of sleep, often make indiscreet remarks with a drink inside them). But until you have done the job you cannot understand what it is really like in there, and how even the most robust supply of self-love and chippiness gets worn down by the curious hours and by the sweat and monotony and alarums of daily current affairs. Once, a young reporter was set to co-present with me during one of the chaps' holidays, and when I reached across to scribble a correction on his cue — I think it was the 'singing' of a treaty, another common pitfall in those days of typewriters and sleepy secretaries — he was furious, and accused me afterwards of patronizing him. My jaw dropped. I tried to make him understand that when the job goes on and on week after week, you have to help one another or all go under.

The other common legend, which surfaces

occasionally when newspapers decide it is time to round up some victimized females, is that as a woman in the seventies I was given 'a hard time' by the two male presenters. Again, I find this vaguely mystifying. It honestly never occurred to me: I was not yet thirty and aware of how much about current affairs I did not know; if the others, particularly Brian, had reason to know more, I deferred to their experience. If — as occasionally happened — I really knew more about a particular story, I said so. Loudly. Sometimes I won. We teased one another, reassured one another, and if I thought Brian was being patronizing or John unnecessarily grumpy, like any normal adult colleague I took the piss out of them until they stopped.

And they retaliated. Brian particularly enjoyed a moment when we were all asked to the Christmas party at Conservative Central Office, and I arrived with a scruffy duffel-coat over my party dress. I got swept to one side by security staff, and made to stand with a deputation of Jobless Youth. 'Yes, yes, Mrs Thatcher will come and have a word with you in a moment,' the aides kept saying, while I bleated, 'Look, I'm a guest, I'm a *Today* presenter, honest.'

Later, when they let me in, Brian could hardly contain his merriment.

15

Off the Bench and on the Road

The studio, the office and the hospitality room were our morning world. People came to us and were given doughy croissants and tinny-tasting coffee; or else they spoke down lines and over radio-car signals. We watched them change, over the years: backbenchers becoming junior ministers, ministers becoming wearier then falling into opposition again and perking up no end (I remember noticing the sheer health contrast between Merlyn Rees as Home Secretary — white as a sheet — and the same man appearing months later in opposition, chipper and spry, while the new Home Secretary Jim Prior drooped). We heard of huge events, and were moved by them even as we struggled to make sense of the reports and pass the news on to the nation. On the morning that John Lennon was shot, one of the night editors was so overcome that he spent the next few hours playing 'Imagine' down the phone to his wife.

We presenters lived, for most of the time, in what would now be called a virtual world. Physical incident was confined to the few delightful occasions when guests fell off the defective banquette in the hospitality room. One of its three supporting legs was wonky at one end, so if a presenter on the far end of the see-saw jumped up suddenly to rush in and back-announce Thought for the Day, anyone perched on the duff end would slither into the waste-paper basket. In one particularly good week we got the Bishop of London, Michael Heseltine and Miss UK. Another time a Northern Ireland Secretary fell in when I jumped up off my end to get back in the studio. His bodyguard (convinced I had knifed the minister) pinned me to the wall. I only just got free in time to introduce Thought for the Day.

I had a little more exercise than the men did, since there was no Ladies' lavatory on the floor where our studio was. Had I been more easily offended I suppose I would have made feminist capital out of this, but as it was I took the chance to pump up my heartrate by running up and down stairs during the News. But we all had outbreaks of stir-craziness in the studio, and would seize gratefully on any opportunity to present the programme from distant parts. It reconnected us with our roots as reporters. It revived for me, in particular, the romantic passion for outside broadcasts; I specially liked OBs involving vans and tangles of cable and surly but expert BBC engineers of the old school.

Outings came in three broad types: party conferences, European summits, and special jobs. Dividing up the conferences was easy. John Timpson did the Tories, Brian did Labour (still in power, for the first nine months of the revived programme). I was sent to the Liberals. The routine was set. With your producer, you hung around some echoing seaside hotel trying to drum up enough stories to fill your section of the programme. At the Liberal Conference this was easy, since there were acres of general humane causes and plenty of New-Agey special interest stands advocating meditation, vegetarianism, or equal rights for transsexuals in women's prisons. There was also Cyril Smith, the vast and opinionated Liberal MP who came in to our studio at dawn and recited a spoof on 'Albert and the Lion' which he had written for the conference. At the Labour Conference Brian would have a lovely time asking long, complicated, glittering questions of excitable MPs, and at the Tory beanfeast John would harrumph along with Lord Carrington.

The second, slightly more exotic type of outing was the Euro-summit. Here I have to admit I was outmanoeuvred. Any meeting which took place in a warm southern European capital with good wine would somehow be snapped up by John or Brian, while I sat at home in the studio saying 'Over now to Rome'. When it was Luxembourg in mid-winter, I got sent there. Still, it was interesting. Mrs Thatcher was just getting into her stride saying '*Non! Non! Non!*' to her fellow-leaders in Europe, and the tension was high. The role of us reporters was to hang around in a vast hall waiting for some gap in the talks, whereon national spokesmen would come out to deliver scraps of news to their compatriot press. It was awful being British because Bernard Ingham, the PM's gruff Yorkshire press secretary, would tell us very little but in a tantalizingly portentous and long-winded way. It was far better to pretend to be Belgian, which was fine for me because I spoke French from my Lille convent childhood. They spilled all the beans and gave us plenty of detail about the shouting and table-thumping. The few British journalists who understood Italian learned even more.

Then, in the morning, you went into an icy little studio at the back of nowhere, hooked yourself up to the programme, and tried to sound as if it was a dynamically interesting event. The editors always pleaded for 'colour'. Once, I slipped over on the polished floor and Mrs Thatcher walked over me, peering down to say, 'Are you all right?' so I asked the day editor whether I should mention this excitement. 'Only,' he said, 'if you saw her underwear.' I didn't.

My other memorable Euro-summit was in Dublin, where I finally rebelled, refusing to join my producer colleagues in sitting on the floor of Bernard Ingham's hotel room till 3 a.m. after the evening session. 'I've got to be properly awake in the morning,' I said. 'He never bloody tells us anything, anyway.' So I retired to bed after dinner with a copy of *Cold Comfort Farm* and a large whisky. In the morning I came downstairs to find Rona Christie, the producer, and Dominick Harrod, the economics correspon- dent, standing together ready to head for the studio.

'OK,' I said, 'so what did finally happen in the talks last, night?'

They replied simultaneously. Rona said,

223

'Nothing!' and Dominick squeaked, 'Crisis!'

Eventually they explained that the very fact that nothing had been agreed represented, in Dominic's view, a crisis. So we reported it as such. God knows what they were arguing about: the Common Agricultural Policy, probably. Dom used to explain it to me once a week regularly, but it seemed too mad to understand. It still does.

Then we would get out and about, interviewing Irish farmers thrilled with the EC's munificence; remembering those days made me grimace thirty-two years later, when a booming Ireland voted in its referendum to pull the ladder up after it and not allow the Polish and East European poor the same grace that they once enjoyed.

Above all, though, the excitement lay not in staged summits or even the ultimate political high of Election Night, when we broadcast for nine hours and emerged so crazed that more than one of us walked straight into a lamp-post. Best of all were the occasional special programmes from abroad. The idea of taking the programme where the action was, with all the freedom and agility that radio could provide, had finally gripped the BBC establishment's imagination. We were not yet geared up with the technology to whip a presenter away at short notice and be sure of getting the report back; a little later on, after the Toxteth riots and the Lockerbie crash, the team would do this with dazzling speed. But presenters were sent abroad for general programmes built around set-pieces: like the talks in Salisbury as Rhodesia became Zimbabwe, or the American presidential primaries.

I covered the Ronald Reagan primary, when it was becoming apparent that he might well become President. It was a fascinating preview of the Reagan years, as I had the chance to talk to his old colleagues in Sacramento about his work habits (one side of A4 per briefing, and no guarantee he'd read that). It was even more fascinating to look out his old Hollywood chums.

I also — because of my French — covered the election of President Mitterrand in Paris. For this I developed a novel new system of vox-pop interviews: ask the question in English, then rattle it off in French, then translate the French answer as soon as you hear it. It was a brain-boiling exercise, but it worked. As the editor of the day said, 'It gives the impression one understands French.' Interviewing French politicians was even more brain-boiling: that was when I came to understand how much more cerebral they are than British ones. French leaders and civil servants are appallingly bright and well-educated veterans of the *Grands Ecoles*. British ones are nearer to the ground, up from the Trades Unions or the narrow, clubbish world of the law. They are, frankly, easier to manage. The French ones had me sweating. So did the celebrations on the street the night Mitterrand won. It was the revolutionary *carmagnole* all over again, and quite a relief that nobody got guillotined.

I also did the programme one day live from

HMS *Invincible*, in the Channel. This was entirely the idea of its commander, Captain Livesey, who rather fancied a live *Today* from his deck and talked the Ministry of Defence into inviting us. As Wrens did not yet serve at sea, they had to get special permission for a woman to be aboard, which caused much naval giggling. I sailed with them the day before, and recorded my quota of interviews all over the ship, about aspects of its life and weaponry. Late in the afternoon I was standing on the Admiral's Bridge alongside the First Officer of the Fleet, watching Sea Harriers take off from a futuristic upswept ramp.

'Funny,' I said, 'that they never sort of bang into the sticking-out bit, and trip over.'

Whereon one did. There was an awful silence as the little plane vanished under the waves, and we looked up to see whether the pilot had ejected. He had.

The Admiral said: 'So sorry — just give me a moment,' and vanished to the main bridge. The producer and I stood there with our mouths hanging foolishly open. Eventually the Admiral reappeared and said: 'Pilot's been picked up fine. You'll be wanting to do a piece for your six o'clock, I suppose? It's the first Harrier we've ever lost this way. D'you mind if we just tell the Ministry first?'

We were gobsmacked. We had expected a total clampdown, possibly the cancellation of the live programme. We were, after all, at their mercy. Besides, we suspected that at least a few of the ship's company would be old-fashioned enough to put the very expensive mishap down to the unlucky presence of a woman on board. But not a flicker: the Navy were cool as cucumbers. I reported the problem in to the six o'clock News down their radio equipment, and we went on setting up the programme for the morning. That night the ship's newsletter carried a long, flippant poem about the disaster including the lines:

> *In front of Auntie Libby*
> *And Uncle FOF, and all . . .*

Nor was our testing of naval cool yet over. Captain Livesey, who by now had got the bit well and truly between his teeth, decided to show off by arranging for a rendezvous with two auxiliary ships and for a RAS (refuelling at sea) to take place actually during the live programme. It never ceases to amaze me how ready people are to set up TV-style spectaculars for radio microphones that can't see a thing. I suppose they appreciate how radio conveys the excitement even though it can't relay the sights. So there we were, at 5.55 a.m., trussed up with lines and pipes to ships alongside, steaming at 20 knots down-Channel, and the producer in London said to me, 'Hey — can you get the ship to hoot Good Morning to John and all our listeners?'

Flinching, I asked the Captain. He considered.

'If I hoot once,' he said, 'the RAS ships either side will turn sharp to starboard, and make a hole in our port side. If I hoot twice, they will turn sharp to port . . . '

Could he not, I muttered, tell them to pay no attention for once?

Graciously, he agreed, and hooted bang on cue. It was a very local-radio sort of moment.

★　★　★

But the cream of all the trips, the one I was luckiest to get, was China. Aubrey Singer had become fascinated by the place since the end of the Gang of Four, the loosening-up of 1978 and the ending of formal worship of Mao's cultural revolution. Democracy Wall, covered in daring graffiti, was flourishing in Beijing: the massive ancient land seemed ready to flower into the twentieth century.

Singer negotiated carefully with Chinese broadcasting, and eventually got an invitation to send a *Today* presenter and do half the programme from China for two mornings in the autumn of 1979. It meant being there for two-and-a-half weeks gathering material; I got the job. On the Monday morning we would have a particularly piquant programme with John Timpson in Dublin for the Papal visit, Brian Redhead in Margate with the Liberal Party Conference, and me in Beijing. Satellites were negotiated with difficulty, and we prepared to make a piece of radio history. It was not only the first ever live news programme from inside China, but the first live programme *in* China. They were still so buttoned-up that they pre-recorded their news bulletins.

Steve Rose and I flew out to Hong Kong, then travelled by train into China. At the border the trashy, flashy neon Coca-Cola culture of Hong Kong stopped abruptly, and we were in an austere and careful land, reminiscent of wartime Britain. Even the station waiting-room chairs had darned antimacassars over their faded backs. Our interpreters met us: Shing Si-Ling, who was greying and thin and serious, and Mr Wong, who was young and larky and a little bit nervous. We had put in a vast list of requests, having been warned by the experienced China correspondent Philip Short that most of them would be refused. But the stops were pulled out for us. Only one — the interview with the Foreign Minister — was refused. The China Broadcasting Administration, evangelical in its desire to open up, had cut through thickets of bureaucracy to get us permissions rarely or never granted to Western journalists before: we would visit a prison, a reform school, the embryonic motor industry, farms, communities, even the office of Vice-Premier Wang Zhen, for an interview on the tricky topic of democracy.

We had our heavy Uher tape recorder and a spare; we had a bagful of razor blades and sticky tape to edit in our hotel room on the little machines, so that we could present proper finished features to the programme. We learned to listen politely as our nervous interpreters fended off eager questions with rote remarks about 'The Four Modernizations', which had now replaced the Gang of Four as the supreme concept. Within a couple of days, we had adapted the whole grammar of our trade — informal radio reportage — to suit the stiffnesses of Chinese bureaucracy.

To take a simple example, that of an interview with a politician or an official. The cult of Politician-as-Favourite-Uncle did not belong to China. When we actually met the Vice-Premier the occasion was so hedged about with courtesies, spare officials, cups of green tea, hot towels and written answers that it was hard to remember the actual questions, and eventually we had to accept that we would get nothing new. With lesser officials there was a different technique to learn: humility. You could not ask a school head or community leader 'What do you do about teenage pregnancy?' or a factory manager 'Do you have problems with absentee-ism?' because the answer would be 'In China, is no such problem.' Instead, I would begin: 'In our country — which has many problems — there is sometimes a situation where workers do not come to the factory/young girls have babies . . . ' Deep breath, expression of sorrow. 'If that ever happened in China, what would you do?'

At this point a grin would split the interviewee's face, and you would get a straight answer. 'Yes, it does happen, and we criticize them . . . '

Straight answers came faster from ordinary people: villagers showing off their pigs, old ladies giggling in helpless laughter at the idea that we had running water and electricity in the house, teenage girls and matrons who ran down the road after me begging to have a look at my bra

230

because they had never seen one. We had to explain to our guides about the British journalistic cult of the average, of the man on the Clapham omnibus: show us a social initiative and we look around instinctively for an Ordinary Bloke to comment on it. It is not a wholly unhealthy instinct, but the Chinese didn't get it at all. We would have to say: 'No, we don't want a model worker or a cadre; yes, we know this girl is only an apprentice, but she is young and pretty and we need to ask what a clothes-factory worker feels about the new dress freedoms . . . oh, please, could we stop by the rice-field and ask those men what they think about the new system of fixes and guarantees which the agricultural bureau officials so kindly explained to us?'

Children in schools were lined up to recite: 'Welcome, Foreign Uncles and Auntees' to us, and once a small boy was pushed forward, grinning widely, to deliver a song entitled, 'I Grow Up in a Communist Garden'. But they giggled like any children, and their teachers clustered round us to compare notes, excitedly, about primary education in Britain. Once, a woman doctor wept as she told us of the exaltation she felt when the isolation of the Maoist cultural revolution finally ended, and doctors were once more allowed to find out what advances science had made in the West. 'We knew about X-rays but not about scanning — and in cancer, in anaesthetics, it is wonderful to know what medicine can do now.'

We did all right. We began to get a scrapbook

of Chinese hopes, worries, laughter and passions (including some brave political dissidents) to relay to the British audience. We began also to accept that there was some good in the political ideologies which had carried the country this far. One day, under a brilliant blue sky at the mountain pass of Padaling, we found ourselves walking along the top of the Great Wall of China — legend, symbol, cliché, wonder of the world. Mr Shing, happier and more at ease than we had yet known him, turned to me as we walked and began to quote Mao-Tse-Tung:

The sky is high, the clouds are pale
We watch the wild geese fly south until they vanish
We count the leagues we have come already.
If we fail to reach the Great Wall we are not true men.

We walked on, under the high pale sky. Shing went on talking. 'For Mao and the Red Army, it was a Long March from the south to reach the Great Wall. For the people of China today the march continues, to achieve the Four Modernizations of our country.' His eyes shone. Softened by the majestic blues and greens of the peaks, chastened by the immensity of the Wall, I had for a moment the educative sensation of accepting the clichés of propaganda at face value. Watching the great grey dragon-back of the Wall climbing out of sight over the hills, I understood the vision of the Long March from starvation to sufficiency and beyond; saw how it might be to feel that the sick man of Asia was standing up at last, a decaying corrupt Confucianism revitalised, adapted, to become a Communist ideal of self-denial and common striving.

'Look, and see what works in the system,' said a young liberal Chinese, back from the LSE. 'When I first went to your country, I didn't believe that such a system could work — everyone pursuing individualism and their own profit, it must be anarchy. Then I saw that, OK, with its faults, it does work. Maybe not for us, not quite like that, but for you, jolly good, fine. In the West you are discontented because you compare horizontally, and complain you are not as rich as the Americans or the Germans. Here, we compare vertically; we are richer than our fathers and will build more prosperity still for our children.'

Of course I knew about human rights violations, industrial problems, corruption, imposed family limits, class unease, and the chafe of the socialist yoke on innocent shoulders. We reported those too. Of course, ten years on from our visit, the enchanting eight year olds in cadre schools who sang to us were eighteen-year-old students being mown down by tanks in Tienanmen Square. But I still maintain that in a country driven by ideology it does no harm to let yourself see the vision for a moment. The currency of idealism, I wrote at the time, 'is so debased in the West that while it is fatal to believe all you are told in any country, for the modern traveller there is a grave danger of believing too little, laughing off every slogan and

233

doubting every good intention. You can't begin to understand what a nation is, until you share its vision of what it wishes that it was.'

Anyway, we had a few meals out, and Philip Short, the ever-obliging China correspondent, got his revenge for being invaded by ignorant London staff by tricking me into eating a sea-slug and a slice of Pekinese dog. We got on the air with a posse of fascinated Chinese broadcasters watching behind the glass; and in the middle of the programme I had a genuine Chinese moment.

I was listening on headphones — with the usual eerie two-second satellite delay — while Brian Redhead nattered knowingly to Simon Hoggart at the Liberal Assembly in Margate. Hoggart said, 'Of course, what they hope is that Mrs Thatcher will start to wobble,' and then John Timpson weighed in with a joke about an MP swimming in the sea; and the sheer disrespect of it staggered me for a second, as I thought my authentic Chinese thought: '*Oh! How can they speak so disrespectfully about their leaders?*'

Then, of course, it all fell into place, and I snapped back into Western, cynical mode. When I got home for my first morning back, Brian Redhead suddenly turned to me in the last seconds of the programme and asked without notice: 'Libby, you're back from China, how does it actually feel to be back? What strikes you about this country?'

And I answered, straight from the heart without thinking: 'How rich we are, and how much meat we eat.'

So, naturally, I got an indignant letter the next day along the lines of, 'Rich? Do you know what the old-age pension is for a retired Brigadier like myself?' and I knew that I was back in carping bloody England again.

16

Gone Tomorrow

By the middle of 1981, after over three years on *Today*, I began to realize that it could not go on forever. Not for me, anyway. The teething troubles with the Controller of Radio 4 were over, and Monica Sims had more or less stopped grumbling about me. I was writing quite a lot of freelance articles as well as presenting the programmes. Paul, who by now was my husband, had given me one invaluable piece of advice about what to do with the modest celebrity that my job brought. 'If it gives you a chance to *do* something,' he said, 'do it, as long as it's difficult. Just don't go with the easy stuff.'

So if a magazine like the *Listener* or the *Spectator* asked me to write something spinning off from my job, I said yes. Whereas if someone wanted to name a rose after me at the Chelsea Flower Show (incredibly, they did) I said no. I would make speeches, but not open supermarkets; earn extra money doing media training, which involved thought and effort, but not accept free dresses to wear at media parties. Not that a *Today* presenter went to many parties; the early hours made it too likely that you would disgrace yourself by falling asleep on some A-list shoulder, or keel over face-down in the pudding at an Inns of Court dinner (actually, I did that once, Middle Temple, since you ask, and a personal injury lawyer nudged me just before my nose hit the duo-demousses).

All the same, I was a bit uneasy about the status which my job conferred. I knew that it was actually not that hard, not nearly as intellectually taxing as being a current affairs producer nor as dangerous and original as being a reporter in the field. Yet presenters got a certain respect, deference even, which was absurdly unearned. You became an institution. I felt as if I was metamorphosing into the Albert Memorial at only thirty-one.

Also, I was starting to be fed up with having to know three minutes' worth about every subject in the world news but never going any deeper; and very jaded with predictable confrontations where you put Clive Jenkins of the TUC in one corner and someone from the CBI in the other, and just let them biff each other for three minutes before winding the session up. Worst of all, I was so often asked 'What time do you get up in the morning?' that the answer was starting to bore me dreadfully, and there is nothing in the world worse than boring yourself.

To liberate myself from ennui, I took on some radio documentaries. Ted Gorton — one of the day editors — was also in search of new stimuli, so he and I made a historical documentary about Edmund Campion called *For Discharge of my Conscience*. We tooled around the priest-hole at Stonor Park with young Lord Camoys (later the Lord Chamberlain), and Ted became so charmed with his new status as a 'real' Radio 4 producer rather than a high-speed hack that he invented himself a middle name. He signed all the recording reports 'Edward St John Gorton'.

Then I managed to blag myself a chance to go out to Oman on behalf of both domestic and world services, and live for a week with the work-party of the explorer Tim Severin, who was building an Arabic ship — with Indian shipwrights — called *Sohar*, to follow the voyages of Sindbad the Sailor. It was wonderful: the muezzin calling on the shore, the ship stinkingly greased with mutton-fat, the romantic pointed mountains of Arabia in the distance, the Indian shipwrights chattering and singing as they worked, relaxed about the microphone because it meant nothing to them. Brokenly, they explained how much it meant to them to ply their dead craft again after long bored years in cardboard-suitcase factories.

The Arab boys gradually thawed from their natural suspicion of a Western woman, and told me their hopes and dreams; and at last, all together, we felt the creak and bubble of power as the great ship got under way beneath the spiky mountains. I read the Koran, thought about my own time on the Atlantic and how star navigation began with the Arab travellers in this desert. I wrote out a verse: 'He it is who hath appointed for you the stars, that you guide yourselves thereby in the vastnesses of land and sea; He hath made the signs distinct for a people which hath knowledge.'

On the negative side the trip also gave me the unique experience of interviewing a sheikh while standing up. He lounged, his male aides lounged, but I as a woman had to stand in his presence, holding the microphone out towards him. I was not pleased at this arrangement, but have always believed in expediency and did not fancy being arrested. So I just muttered the old Arab proverb, which is also ideal for those moments when you find yourself silently at odds with some BBC mandarin: 'The camel driver has his thoughts, and the camel he has his . . .'

I asked Ken Goudie to reduce my days on the programme to three a week; they began to experiment with putting John and Brian together for two days. I made a programme about Frank Muir's book collection. I did a long interview for the Sound Archives with my heroine Stella Gibbons, author of Cold Comfort Farm, and found her to be so brilliant a talker even in extreme old age that we made it into a half-hour programme. I wrote more and more, travelling on a Trinity House tender, a tug and a cargo ship for the Observer magazine. I got together a book of my Punch pieces, Britain at Play. I wondered whether perhaps it was time to have a baby, and got a fertility thermometer to see when my temperature rose (though at 4 a.m. I appeared to be clinically dead most days).

There was one more bit of outside-broadcast fun to come: the wedding of Prince Charles and Lady Diana Spencer. It was the last of the great royal occasions, the last time the nation hypnotized itself into believing that there was something special, magical, and invulnerable about a princely wedding. We were all, despite our better judgement ('God! She's too young!'), swept up in what the Archbishop of Canterbury disingenuously called 'the stuff of which fairy tales are made'. As an aficionado of outside broadcasts and the complex technical magic of radio, I have kept the fifty-page technical briefing written by the day's producer, Trevor Taylor (who now runs *Gardeners' Question Time*). It is a wonderful document. Although our time only ran from 0600 till 0839 that July morning, and the wedding was not until much later in the day, we were all over the streets of London like a rash.

Brian Redhead was in the studio, John Timpson with a mobile unit trundling along the processional route to St Paul's; I was positioned among the crowds on the Strand, outside Bush House with a microphone on a long wire and a constant supply of woffle from James Whitaker of the *Mirror*, who worshipped Diana already. Elsewhere no fewer than seventeen reporters had such specialist tasks as reporting from the fireworks-makers, harassing the builders of the wedding-dress, lurking in St Paul's, and staking out Althorp Park. There are over fifty engineers and assistants named on the document, and little gems of stage-management — 'Andy Price will select interesting members of the public, encourage them to be humorous and even sing' . . . 'Libby will capture the flavour of the wait' . . . 'Chief Petty Officer Cook Fraser of HMS *Pembroke* in Chatham will enter Buckingham Palace at 0800 to repair any damage to the cake . . . and will talk to John Timpson'.

Logistically, it was a masterpiece. I doubt Trevor ever had such a challenge before or since. It all went off smoothly, though I got slightly fed up with my position on the Strand and thought of nipping up the road to help Andy Price get the Trafalgar Square crowds singing.

But even on that day there was something less fresh about my job than there had once been. I was withdrawing, little by little, from *Today*. Friends on the production side were moving over to breakfast television. In the autumn a new editor came, Julian Holland, and before I even saw him I had made up my mind. My first dealing with him was to hand in my notice: or rather say that I had decided not to renew my contract at the end of November, after three and a half years as presenter.

The response from him and the department head was in the worst sort of BBC style — brusque, graceless, and accompanied by an insistence that I work until the end of December as that 'would be more convenient'. Mindful of that private moment six years earlier when I had resolved to have clients rather than masters, I told them that I would stay until the ninth, and that was my best offer. My editor barely spoke a word to me after that, except in late-January when I was trying to get paid (two months late) for the extra shifts, and he informed me rather sneeringly that I was lucky to have any work and would do well not to antagonize the BBC as 'It's bigger than you are.'

I think they were mainly annoyed that I had not allowed the BBC press office to get in first with the announcement of my going. I had given the story to a newspaper diary and written a piece in *Punch* about it. This was because, much as I loved the BBC, I also knew it rather well and did not trust it any further than I could throw it. The Corporation would have been quite capable of putting out a weaselling story suggesting that I had been sacked. Anyway, Julian Holland and I were clearly never going to be soulmates, so I was glad to be leaving. It should be noted in fairness, though, that he proved a cracking good editor from the programme's point of view and saw it most triumphantly through the Falklands War.

I did my last shift on Wednesday, 9 December. It felt like being written out of *The Archers*, or killed off in Coronation Street. The indignation of the letters (and the Controller) which had accompanied my arrival three and a half years earlier was matched only by the indignation of the letters (and the very same Controller) at the fact that I was going. People get used to radio voices and are annoyed by their sudden removal. 'How could you walk out on us,' demanded one listener, 'with Christmas barely a month away?' I realized that, like Robinson and de Manio before me, I had become as familiar and taken-for-granted by regular listeners as a seedy old pair of pom-pom slippers or a dog-gnawed hot water bottle.

But I was not quite thirty-two. It really was time to get out from under; every day strengthened that conviction. So the last programmes ticked by; the last party conference,

242

the last by-election, the last ho-ho with Timpson, the last M6 lane closure, and the last wave of nausea at nine o'clock, a time when the breakfastless body is so saturated with bad coffee that it feels like a terrible brown sponge beneath the skin. (Brian and I used to say that if any normal person felt the way we did at nine in the morning, they'd call the doctor. How he kept on going through the years when he really was ill, I cannot imagine.)

Then there was the last time signal, the last scuffle through eight newspapers in forty minutes, the last sighting of Roy Hattersley. Brian and I worked out that I had done 9,384 timechecks over the years. I knew I would miss it all: the round of brief encounters, the regular stage army of newsreaders, sportscasters, invisible crackling foreign correspondents, jolly bishops thinking their Thoughts, Gloria from Grenada, the cleaning lady, unshaven political correspondents, and a host of experts on everything under the sun, taxied in from the *Observer* or the *FT*, from *Sea Trade* and *Jane's Fighting Ships* and the Institute of Strategic Studies and the CBI and the *Jewish Chronicle* and *Flight International*.

And then it was all over. I cleaned out my locker and said goodbye to the few friends who still worked on the programme. They were so hopelessly disorganized, disoriented by the hours and the new editor and the competition from breakfast TV, that I never even got a farewell card, something which it took me twenty years to get over properly. I had signed dozens of the damn' things over the years, after all. However, it later turned out (at one of the noisy reunion lunches which sporadically occur) that there had been a card after all, signed by everyone. But one of the reporters forgot about it, and found it months later in the bottom of his briefcase.

And why should I carp? On that programme I had more fun than fun. I am glad that I left when I did; I would not have been as happy with the obsessively political, talking-head direction that it took in later years. I like light and colour and atmosphere and wit and insight more than I like headline-making rows and remorseless 'agenda-setting'.

But it did feel, on that last day, as if I stood on a strange quay with my kitbag while the old packet weighed anchor and steamed back to sea without me. To misquote Sylvia Plath, resigning is an art: I do it exceptionally well, I do it so it feels like hell.

17

The Sound and the Story

I had work under way, although nowhere near enough to live on. In December I finally finished a complicated documentary called *Street Gospel* which had taken months of collecting to make. I dreamed it up one day near home, in Deptford, while edging my way round a group of gospel-singers in the market. Some New Testament line came to me about taking the Word out into the highways and byways; and after a rather cathedral-heavy High Anglican summer, with Lord Runcie in his gilded robes conducting the Royal Wedding, it occurred to me to wonder how much street evangelism survived in Britain. Where were the heirs of Bunyan and Wesley? Was there still a role for the ancient simplicities of the stepladder and the soap-box?

I took the idea to the radio religious department, who allotted me the Reverend John Newbury as producer. I told him — as often as possible — that this arrangement was like doing a natural history programme produced by a real live badger. Between us we drew up lists of gospellers and where to find them. I stalked Lord Soper in Hyde Park and at Tower Hill, with a microphone concealed in my woolly hat at his request ('The hecklers get even sillier, if they see a microphone or a camera'), and marvelled at the patience and power of this man, who continued to preach international peace and social justice when confronted with nutters shouting, '*WOSSAT? Yer keep goin' on abaht Israel, sod bloody Israel, wot abaht the price of a meat pie? We've had enough of your Christian-diabolical rubbish, Soper, you old git. Get back to Wales and burn dahn a few more houses with the rest of yer bleeding Welsh mates . . .* ' I transcribe, exactly.

John Newbury worked his local High Street and found gospellers forlornly shouting, 'It's not too late for you to be saved, unhappy people of Sydenham!' I caught some brave young girl Christians staking out the dirty-film cinemas in Leicester Square ('Yes, I'm terrified, but Jesus *died* for us . . . '); John found a trainee Baptist minister in a comic bowler hat in the park balancing a banana on his nose, and I chugged along the Norfolk Broads with a Church Army mission group. We interviewed a sandwich-board man who for forty-nine years has toured Britain labelled FLEE THE WRATH TO COME, and I waited one Sunday in a dull Sheffield sidestreet for the brass and glory of the Salvation Army.

The cacophony, the tapestry of sound we collected, was wonderful. It made my mouth water at the very thought of editing and weaving it together, as I had done years before on Radio Oxford. I gloried in being free from the desperate topicality of the current affairs department, and being able to admit that something which is interesting now can still be interesting in a month's time. To top it off we found a holy and intense Welshman who had actually been converted by a billboard on Swansea station, and grilled one of the London bishops about why street gospellers are never mainstream Anglicans or Catholics who direct you to the nearest branch of an established Church. 'I suppose we're shy,' he said, nervously.

Assembling all this was a joy. I got on very well with the religious department of those days, mainly under the Reverend David Winter, and often did a stint presenting the *Sunday* programme for them. This was their equivalent of *Today*, and I found it bracing to be able to ask religious questions about current affairs — like asking Orange Lodge drum-bangers 'What about Blessed are the Meek, then?' or demanding to know why so-called Catholic bombers felt exempted from the fourth commandment. *Street Gospel* was followed by *Electric Gospel*, about tele-evangelists in the USA and their aim to come to Britain; then by a biography of Teresa of Avila and one of my favourite documentaries ever, *Holy Bones*, about the cult of relics.

This had its origin in a silly office conversation with John Newbury about how General Franco used to have St Teresa of Avila's dried hand on his bedside table, when someone else chipped in about a French monastery which claimed to have the foreskin of Christ.

'Gosh,' I said. 'We have it in our power to make the worst-taste religious programme *ever*.'

So we trotted in to David Winter's office, giggling, to share the joke and he said, 'Go on

247

then, make it.' He knew that John was a clergyman and I was not a fool, saw that the subject of relics was generally intriguing, and assumed that we would balance it and treat real belief with real respect. That was the joy of the pre-Birt BBC. Departments had programme slots in their gift; people close to the reporters and producers (and to the subject) could make snap decisions and stand by them. From the second David said 'Yes' we were up and running, enthusiasm still intact. We did one A4 sheet of 'proposal' for his desk drawer, and began phoning round, just as you would on a magazine or a newspaper supplement.

Once the system changed under Birt, any such happy idea inevitably led to months or even years of uncertainty, and the need to woo layers of distant 'commissioning editors' with proposals honed more finely than any actual programme. By the mid-nineties you had, in addition, to answer fussy questions concerning theoretical age-appeal, 'reach', and 'inclusivity'. Covert debates would then follow among the cadres about whether the idea should be accepted, but done with a different presenter to 'create a vehicle' for some newspaper or TV celebrity that the network had its eye on. Everyone concerned with the original idea would become depressed and cynical long before the first word was recorded. The same principle applied everywhere in the Corporation throughout the ghastly 1990s: the most notable damage it did on-air was to the quality of radio comedy, but documentary suffered too.

John Newbury and I set off round Britain, found pockets of fervour and touching oddities, related historical gorinesses about pickled saints and fingers being bitten off, got the Bishop of London to confess that he always kept a knee-bone of St Philip Neri in his cassock pocket, and teased the Methodists about disapproving of relics but still preserving John Wesley's boots in a glass case. There were some ringing testimonies — 'In this flesh, a saint lived and breathed and had his being' — and again I was struck by how wonderfully apt the medium of radio is for matters of faith, belief, ethics and spirituality. You listen to the words, humanized by the voice and breath; but you are not distracted by the funny glasses or the suit you would not be seen dead in. Radio offers just enough of a speaker's personality, without swamping the meaning of his or her words.

Just as I left *Today*, I had actually been offered seventeen weeks' work by the religious department, hosting an audience and panel show called Choices. I have always liked public meetings and question-times and debates; the subjects were wide and fascinating. The only drawback was that this job was on TV.

Every interesting aspect of it — the impassioned speakers, some ordinary and some celebrities (from Kenneth Williams to Fay Weldon), the serious subjects ranging from euthanasia to arranged marriages, the ability to flit round the audience picking up comments and rants — was really a staple of radio. Putting it on television added nothing but irritation, as far as I was concerned. If it's the thoughts that count, why must people have faces to stare at?

And, God help us, clothes. I was forced to go to Dickins & Jones with a wardrobe lady to buy some 'little tops', all very Thatchery and pussycat-bow — and bullied into wearing lipgloss. Moreover, there was a ridiculous nonsense about my glasses. I had worn contact lenses for years because they are less trouble and I can see better: needing keen peripheral vision to look round the auditorium, I assumed that on Choices I would wear them as usual. But one day, the head of the TV department responsible walked into the office and saw me in my glasses because I had lost a lens; and his tiny TV mind conceived an idea: specky intellectual woman . . . something different . . . kinda Nana Mouskouri look . . . boing!

So he demanded that I wear glasses on-air. 'They give you such *authority*!' he said.

I wore them for two weeks. Black-rimmed, very severe. Then there was a review-board meeting full of tremendously senior TV suits, which apparently devoted nearly half its length to discussing whether the glasses were right or not. Never mind whether our debate on abortion had been any good: it was the presenter's glasses that mattered to them. And the outcome was that the same creep came back and asked me to wear contact lenses.

So I did. And after the first programme in contacts, he breezed in and gushed: 'Great! With your glasses you had authority. Without them, Libby, you have authority *and charm!*', I think it

250

was then that I realized television would never be for me.

I have nothing against pictures: since that time I have done countless voice-overs for documentaries or rewritten commentaries to film. But never again did I voluntarily step in front of a camera, except as a quiz show participant or when forced on to one of those grisly sofa-shows by a book publicist. Next to finding out what you want to do in life, the most useful lesson is to find out what you don't want to do. I might have been happy as a TV reporter, or behind the camera as a film-maker; but never, never, never in that Avon-lady-lipgloss-world of the TV presenter. Choices — where I could at least forget the cameras and just be a chairman — was the nearest I ever got, and even that was pretty painful.

Ironically, much the same had happened to my old oppo John Timpson during his brief encounter with *Tonight*, while he was away from Radio 4. Just in case you are tempted to draw some dull moral from the above about how hard it can be for *women* in television, listen to John. It isn't exclusively hard for women: it's just hard for normally spontaneous people whose vanity is not of the physical kind.

Talking to Paul Donovan for his history of the *Today* programme, Timpers said:

I never really got used to the television world. You were just a sort of little automaton with this thing stuck in your ear telling you when to start, when to stop, which way to look, when to get up

. . . I found it all terribly restricting and worrying and hence I wasn't terribly good at it, I'm afraid. There was a great argument over why did I always have such a schoolboy haircut. I remember getting criticized in the papers and my masters took this immediately to heart and insisted I had to go and have fancy haircuts and blow-waves.

Anyway, I had other preoccupations. I was pregnant, had a book project editing the work of the sailor and climber H. W. Tilman, and needed to get a freelance writing practice going. I had vaguely thought that the BBC would drop me entirely when I left *Today*: there was a curious incident a month later when I had my bag snatched and lost my BBC identity card. It had nearly a year to run, so I asked for a replacement and was told that this was impossible. Had the old one endured, I could have used it. Since it was lost, I would have to be fetched from Reception each day I worked in a BBC building, like any other visitor. They would not even issue me a one-month pass. It was the first time in ten years that I did not have a BBC ID card, and it was a great bore when working on documentaries.

However, other radio jobs trickled in. I did a few editions of *File on Four* out of Manchester, something of which I remain inordinately proud (it remains the benchmark for rigorous, strong, in-depth radio current affairs). In the last months of pregnancy, and then during a cold winter of dragging a snuffling Moses-basket around the country, I chaired an experimental series invented by the Head of Presentation, Jim Black. It was to be just like *Gardeners' Question Time*, only about do-it-yourself. We had a panel of experts, and descended on various draughty halls with straggly thin audiences to answer pressing questions about DIY. I would leave the baby with a local agency nurse in someone's office, just out of earshot but within the short range tolerable to my maternal anxiety. A great many of the questions were about damp chimney-breasts, I remember, and they were not the kind of breasts that were uppermost in my mind. It was all rather surreal.

Two memories stick: one is of the night we reached Plymouth just as the *Sheffield* had gone down in the Falklands War. It was soon plain that under the circumstances nobody in that naval city was going to leave their TV set to come and ask questions about grouting. So the outside broadcast engineers and production secretary had to come out front and invent some, in a variety of different voices, and flesh out the applause and laughter later on in the editing. The other memory is of a long, intense discussion between the panel about a question from a woman who needed to keep dangerous medication very cool, and wanted to know how you could lock a fridge. The experts went on and on about padlock-flanges and rustproof screws until a man in the audience stuck his hand up and said, 'Why not get a lockable cashbox and put the medicine in that, in the fridge?' Quite.

★ ★ ★

I began to do the occasional guest interview — the 'birthday interview' for a programme called *Midweek* on Radio 4. After a while it became a regular weekly thing. I had not done such long interviews live since local radio, and became captivated by this new art. When you are recording for a documentary, or a non-live programme like *Desert Island Discs* or *In the Psychiatrist's Chair*, you sit quiet, let the speaker have long pauses or repeat himself, and just use your questions to prompt. All the while you may be editing it in your head, thinking, 'I'll let him get this off his chest then ask the question again more pointedly.' You let time pass.

When you are live, you can't. This is one of the reasons why live broadcasters get a bad name for 'interrupting', unlike the 'politer' interviewers on recorded programmes. On *Today* the imperative was obvious to all: in those days nothing lasted beyond five minutes (I still find the present-day twenty-minute epics very hard to take at eight in the morning when I want to hear the rest of the news). On a live talk show like *Midweek*, *Woman's Hour*, or *Start the Week*, you have to keep things moving; moreover, you can't leave long gaps of silence because not only does the listener start to worry, but the interviewee becomes embarrassed. If they dry up you must jump in with a question which will help them get going again. If they lose the thread, you find it. If they are drunk, or obscene, or libellous, you handle the situation: not later in an editing room but right now, live on the air. If they are going to overrun their time and use up someone else's, you have to cut them off.

Yet because the interviews had space (*Midweek* was nearly an hour long then, and each guest had over ten minutes) you could achieve quite a strong interview, ask some complex questions or hear some proper anecdotes. And overarching it all was something I had not thought much about before, but which seems to me even more important.

There is an honesty about live interviews. The subject knows that this is now, this is real, their words will not be altered and cut and shifted and twisted and re-emphasized. If they are famous — as birthday guests always were — they have the chance to deny, in real time, directly to the listeners, any old canards or lies which have circulated in the press-cuttings and gossip columns for years. If they are unknown and quite timid, the liveness of the interview often gives them an extraordinary boost of adrenalin and confidence. Like witnesses nerving themselves to give evidence because it matters, they tell their stories all the better for telling them live. The process fascinated me. It still does.

18

Conversation

I did the *Midweek* interviews at first with Henry Kelly as presenter, then served for a spell with Russell Harty. Russell was a joy to work with — far better on radio than on television. He had the unique quality of asking questions as innocently as a four-year-old, and accordingly getting amazingly frank answers. When a small child points at you on a bus and says 'Why've you got big bazoomas?' you don't take offence. There's no point. You just think of an answer. It was much the same with Russell.

He used to sit before the programme, hair rumpled, headphones askew, scribbling and saying, 'What shall I ask first? Oh, dear, what *do* we want to know?' Once, in an outside broadcast from Paris, we had Charlotte Rampling and Jean-Michel Jarre coming, and there was a slight discussion as to whether they counted as one guest or two. 'So that's the first question,' said Russell, scribbling. 'How many of you are there?' After that, it became an existential pre-programme joke. Whenever Russell couldn't think what to ask Chris Bonington, or Mary Whitehouse, or Ravi Shankar, he would say: 'What shall I ask?' and I would reply, 'How many of you are there?' and he would say, 'Deep! Oh, deep!'

I have never forgotten the moment in Mary Whitehouse's interview with him when he listened to a long harangue about purity of the airwaves and then asked vaguely, 'Do you do much cooking these days?' It sounded ingenuous, but in fact the answer — no, she didn't — was curiously illuminating of the fact that while she always claimed to speak as an 'ordinary housewife', she had for years been a full-time and highly professional campaigner.

Another of his great moments was when he got so swept away by the eloquence and descriptive powers of the mountaineer Chris Bonington that he carried on the interview right to the end of the hour, leaving no room for the last guest. 'Ooh, I am sorry,' he said camply to the bewildered figure at the foot of the table. 'Will you come back next week?' Nobody else would have got away with it. Russell Harty was a joy, both then and later on, when he took over *Start the Week*. He is a great loss.

The producer, Peter Estall, wanted me to present *Midweek* when Henry left, but twice came up against opposition from the Controller of Radio 4. After a period of approving of me on *Today* — just as I left, the tide turned — she had now returned to her conviction of four years earlier that I should be strictly a reporter, not a presenter. Owing to the curious way that the BBC worked this blocking was never quite acknowledged: technically a production department had editorial control, but in reality such matters as the choice of presenter were subject to veto from much higher up (just as they were in the days when Lord Reith overruled his music staff and banned a Divorced Woman from singing in a concert). Eventually, bored with the absurdity of it all, I went to beard the Controller in her office.

She welcomed me with practised charm, and seemed baffled at any suggestion that she was stopping me presenting *Midweek*. 'So is Pete lying, then?' I said rather brutally, whereon she explained that, well, the thing was, my documentaries were splendid, she had loved *Street Gospel*, and surely it would be better if I used my talents that way? Patiently I explained that *Street Gospel* had in effect paid about a quid an hour, that documentaries like this for the radio service are a labour of love, and that I couldn't live on them even if I got enough commissions.

'But is that an issue? I mean, you're married,' said the Controller, prized figurehead of women's advancement in the BBC. Oh, dear. Clearly 1955 was one of those years that took a very, very long time to end.

* * *

In the end, I kept the mortgage money rolling in by doing a six-month spell (all I could stand) of working for Condé Nast magazines, editing the *Tatler*. I disliked the magazine but — after years of the BBC — absolutely adored the management structure. If you wanted something done, you asked your boss. If he wouldn't help, you rang the European chairman, slinky Daniel

Salem. If you thought they were both wrong, you could ring Si Newhouse, the owner. And that was that: the top of the tree, the final word. No diffuse grey layers of management, no interlocking directorates, no smoke and mirrors. If only I had not been bored silly by the values of the *Tatler* itself, I could have been happy there. But at least by the time I left it the Controller had relented, and from 1983 to the present day I have presented *Midweek* for forty-five weeks a year, all but a handful of them live.

The commonest misconception is that the presenter 'finds' the guests, or at least has a strong say in who comes on. Wrong. The fact is that, as presenter, I eat what I'm served: a table d'hôte menu which the producer and researcher come up with, four strangers a week. The research is sent over to me on Friday and Monday, so I can read books or watch videos that are relevant. Sometimes, however, the last guest is not confirmed until Tuesday afternoon. I make suggestions, but they are no more or less likely to be taken up than anyone else's. The guests come from anywhere and everywhere. A few are there because they have a book or film out, but the majority flow in from other directions: a topical link, a producer's whim, an anniversary or birthday, a small but mind-boggling report in a newspaper ('Can this be real? What can they be like? Why do they do it?'). Sometimes they arrive by pure serendipity. One of the most striking guests we ever had was an elderly missionary who had preached the Gospel to the Inuit and lived in an igloo, and who was found by the producer's mother on the WI speaking circuit.

For the first fifteen years or so of my time, before the James Boyle 'reforms' reduced it to forty-three minutes instead of fifty-five, *Midweek* stuck with the old format: the presenter doing three of the interviews, and a guest interviewer for the prime or 'birthday' guest. There was a long period when it was thought entertaining to bring in another celebrity, changing every week, to do the guest interview. Jill Freud interviewed Diana Quick, Bernard Levin did Robin Day (an encounter in which I was devoutly thankful to be spared the full blast of the old warrior's combativeness) and Richard Ingrams did Naim Attallah. It was the first time the latter two met, and although Ingrams grumbles that I kept interrupting him, it was the beginning of a long and fruitful relationship which gave birth to the *Oldie* magazine. Ian Hislop, before his elevation to *Private Eye* editorship and TV stardom, interviewed Jeffrey Archer in a nerve-jangling encounter in which Archer weirdly accused him of being a socialist. In a pleasing departure from his normal instinct towards mayhem, the producer of the day, Victor Lewis-Smith, bleated down the talkback at me, 'Make it all friendly again!'

Some of the celebrity-meets-celebrity guest spots were wonderful, others dreadful. It opened up a whole new interest for the presenter, who had to dive in to rescue interviews which had gone so haywire that both parties were thoroughly miserable, or were confusing the

260

listener so much that something needed to be done. After a while, before the celebrity-cum-interviewer was scrapped entirely, we settled back to using professionals — including John Diamond in the year before he lost his voice — which was easier. One of our star tryouts was James Naughtie from the *Financial Times*. I remember saying to the producer afterwards: 'Wow, he's really got it, hasn't he?' and indeed he went on to be one of the best of the *Today* presenters. I think his quality — right from the start — was that he was more interested in what was being said than in how good he sounded saying it.

Actually, it was never quite fair to expect Fleet Street journalists, however personally brilliant, to catch on straight away to the odd conventions of radio interviewing. It may sound like a normal conversation, yet it is nothing of the kind because it is conducted entirely for the benefit of an invisible eavesdropper behind the arras. I suppose it is a bit like those casual conversations which undercover policemen have with their marks, when they know a team of spooks is lurking behind the building with a satellite receiver on a plain van. You have to sound as if it is just you asking the questions, but really you represent a multitude of listeners who have not read the research, may not automatically be interested in your subject, and know either far less or far more than you do.

Moreover, while on radio you can nod and grimace and smile to encourage a shy speaker, you can't break in with 'yah . . . yah . . . I see

. . . oh!' as you might in normal speech. It's annoying. And you must often ask questions to which you know the answer, and manage to sound surprised and pleased when you get it. On top of it all, you must be prepared to interrupt because the clock is king, and to bow your head resignedly to the fact that a lot of listeners will think you are rude for doing it. These things are obvious, but not always recognized.

The joy of this particular job is the mix, and that is the reason I have been doing it once a week for nineteen years (unless they sack me before this gets through the printing process, which is always a possibility). *Midweek* is often scorned, especially by newspaper columnists and the more depressing radio reviewers, and frequently gets parodied by radio comedians; but the things which are easiest to lampoon are actually its hidden strengths. Never a year passes without some radio sketch show taking the piss: 'And with us today a fairly well-known trouser manufacturer, the Dalai Lama, and the once unknown actress who shot to notoriety as Dinksie in *Emmerdale*.'

I never mind this in the slightest. I agree that *Midweek* as a concept is ludicrous, but on the other hand where else are you going to hear those people interacting: the famous and the unknown, the dedicated and the eccentric, the ordinary and the extraordinary? Where — apart from *Midweek* or a fortuitously stranded lift — might you overhear the late Lord Chancellor, Lord Denning, questioning the Miss UK beauty queen, and enjoy the following

262

unhistoric but pleasing exchange:

'How long do you take to get dressed for a beauty contest?'

'Not long. How long does it take you to get dressed in your judge stuff?'

'Oh, quite a long time, especially with my gold robes and those silk stockings . . . '

In these circumstances the presenter's role is to sit back and keep quiet while things develop, and hope with pious fervour that they get down to detail about suspender belts. It is the reaction of one guest to another that makes the programme work, when it does work (it doesn't always. It couldn't). The producer and researcher who spend all week lining up and writing me notes on the guests have often got themes, common strands or contrasts in mind, but just as often the spark is struck from a wholly unexpected direction when natural enemies turn out to be soulmates or a gulf of antipathy opens up between apparent allies.

I remember how Monty Roberts, the original horse whisperer and survivor of a violent childhood, began to weep quietly, almost losing his ability to talk, as young Lord Linley talked about how much he owed his father, Snowdon. I cherish the memory of the day when after a rather awkward booking week, the rufty-tufty former *Sun* editor Kelvin MacKenzie found himself at a table with a Greenham Common protester, an earnest aid worker, and a former bag lady rehabilitated through religion. When he heard who his companions were, MacKenzie snarled, 'It's a wind-up, is it?' and then relented and said, 'Bloody good wind-up anyway.'

In the event, he got on tremendously with the bag lady, who announced that she shared his views about having a right to live in a nice home, and then he had a wonderful exchange of views with Thalia Campbell, who makes banners for feminist-pacifist demonstrations. She said to him, quite indignantly, that modern tabloids have no news sense, because on the day after a delegation of women left by train for the Women's Summit in Beijing, with colourful banners and great joy, the headlines entirely failed to report it. They were all, she said indignantly, giving priority to Hugh Grant's arrest with a Los Angeles prostitute. 'And who on earth cares about that?' she concluded.

MacKenzie sighed a deep, frightening, editor's sigh and said, 'Madam, you may be very intelligent in your own way but I have to tell you that you do not have a future in newspaper journalism.' I admired his restraint.

Although *Midweek* is mainly a sequence of interviews, with only a few moments of discussion between the guests rather than a set, seminar-style theme, it often seems to me that each interview is changed by the fact of having at the same table three visible listeners. Thus the late Larry Adler gave hundreds of interviews, getting better and better as he grew older, but it was only on one of his visits to *Midweek* that you could have heard the old wit's reaction to a woman boxing MC. There have been many interviews with Cher's rebelliously butch daughter Chastity, but never before had she sat next to

Boy George and heard him sighing with envy about her wasted opportunities to riffle through Cher's make-up drawers as a child.

The Prime Minister's father-in-law Tony Booth is, to my mind, even more interesting to hear when in the company of Julian Clary, a Sioux Indian and a paralyzed ex-pilot who was head boy of Gordonstoun. It was wonderful to watch avant-garde American ballet dancers enjoying the company of the veteran *Carry On* actress and camp icon Joan Sims, an elderly war hero fascinated by a rap artist, and Margaret Cook — at the time the disgruntled former wife of the Foreign Secretary — sharing a platform with a conjurer and a royal dressmaker. The truly good and great spirits of the world, like the South African freedom fighter Albie Sachs or the poet Irina Ratushinskaya, grow even more attractive in incongruous company. Their response, their warmth or amusement or appalled disbelief, is part of the atmosphere. On the other hand, the pompous or insecure find it impossible to remain inside their bubble of self-importance when everyone else is being charmed by the memoirs of a trapeze artist.

Sometimes whole new relationships spring up on the programme: my only claim to street credibility in the whole of the nineties was that Damon from Blur met his new girlfriend across our table. Oh, and that Frank Zappa met Paddy Moloney of the Chieftains, and became his friend. And again, going back to that programme with Lord Linley and Monty Roberts, it is a source of satisfaction to remember how each of them listened with appalled interest to the story of a very ordinary waitress, who had successfully brought a case against her employers after the comedian Bernard Manning racially and sexually abused the serving staff with jokes and the Rotarian hosts joined in the dreadful laughter. She quoted the jokes; any doubt in anybody's mind faded, visibly, from their faces. And next to her again was a released hostage home from Colombia. And then there was the joy of introducing former Chancellor of the Exchequer Denis Healey to the principal and foundress of the London School of Striptease. It is like an extraordinary, condensed dinner-party at nine o'clock in the morning. I love it.

Very occasionally, *Midweek* is allowed out, with an outside broadcast van, to do programmes from elsewhere. Once we went to New York and had Quentin Crisp and Helene Hanff on. There was an awkward moment when the bouffant blue hair of Crisp caused a fellow-guest to shake his hand enthusiastically under the impression he was Ms Hanff. One autumn we toured Britain, doing the programme not in front of audiences (which in my view kills any talk show dead) but in people's front rooms. We broadcast live from Sue Earle's farmhouse in Yorkshire as it crept towards the edge of the cliff before falling into the sea; from a terrace in Hull, with a lady private detective and a champion foster-mother; from a stately home in Lancashire where the icy cold bit into our bones; from a film-animal farm; and from a boarding house in Great Yarmouth, where John Timpson graced us with his presence and an enthusiastic dentist explained why he adores his job because 'you're working on people's smiles'.

There are, of course, killer guests and killer moments. Some fail entirely to respond to the faintly goofy goodwill of the studio and remain wrapped in their own dignity. Some are bullies. Robert Maxwell — just by being there — made everybody else so nervous that they said almost nothing; so did Enoch Powell, though without meaning to. The latter, who came on in the last years of his life, notoriously freaked out the researcher Suzy when she asked (as one must in a building as awkward as Broadcasting House) whether anyone needed the Gents before the programme began. He replied in his high, banshee tones, 'Nohhh . . . I find I speak better on a full bladder.' It is hard to appreciate a joke when you are desperately uncertain as to whether one was intended. Suzy nearly passed out from stress.

Only once has a guest been drunk on the programme; it was awkward because drunkenness does not necessarily make a speaker gay and voluble. More commonly it makes them very slow and deliberate. 'Now, I'm going to make *three* points about that. No, *four*. I tell a lie — only three . . . And the shecond one, I mean the firsht one, is . . . ' etc. Only once has a guest been so furious that he walked out afterwards calling me a 'bitch', and that was an American four-star General. He was annoyed when I challenged his boast that he always made sure his men in Vietnam got 'good clean girls' without diseases.

Only three times in eighteen years has the F-word been spoken. Once it was by Jeremy Irons, who regretted it instantly; once it was sufficiently inaudible to get away with; and once it was said by someone quoting a racist gibe which had been hurled at him. We had a good letter from a listener saying, 'Thank you, Radio 4, for allowing that intelligent and informative use of the expression 'f — king nig-nog'. We have to know how our countrymen behave.'

Normally, people behave very well on live radio. Sometimes almost too well. Normally they are glad to tell their stories, or put their point of view with minimal leading from the presenter. Often I find myself wrapped up in admiration and empathy for the marvellous, creative, courageous diversity of the human race. Only occasionally do I dislike or distrust them. Sometimes I am brought to silence by the raw reality of what they tell me: about being a foster-mother, an FBI sniper, a North Sea diver, a convict.

It is rare, in the context of this programme, that I bother to be combative. This is not *Today*. If someone really is unpleasant or absurd, it is better to hand out coils of rope, gently, and allow them to get on with hanging themselves. I once got a furious letter from a feminist after Sir John Junor said on the programme that he didn't think women should be airline pilots in case they had periods and crashed the plane. I should, said my correspondent, have 'challenged him and told him he was wrong'. Instead of that, I had

268

mildly enquired exactly what he thought it felt like for a woman, when she had a period? The resulting bluster was far more enlightening than anything you get by contradicting someone. I prefer to leave the listener, who is not stupid, to judge how batty the guest might be. When David Attenborough shows you a badger creeping from its hole, he does not shout in best Paxman style 'Why are you so black and white? Why have you got those stupid big paws? My goldfish doesn't use paws like that! A lot of people will be wondering, just what's the point in all this digging?'

No. Attenborough just points, and murmurs very, very quietly 'Look! A badger! If we keep very, very still he might come out where we can see him better . . . '

That's the way to do it.

19

Bad Times

Normally, I keep well out of BBC politics. The most important relationship a broadcaster should have is not with his or her boss, but with the listener. The second most important relationship is with the interviewee, or the subject of the programme. So if you are making a programme — whether about stair-rods, toasted cheese, quantum physics, rap music or Bertrand Russell — you should be joyfully obsessed with stair-rods, toasted cheese, quantum physics, rap music or Bertrand Russell. Not with the whims of your commissioning editor, the policy of your department, the sensitivities of the current government, or the probable reaction of some dismal sourpuss in the Sunday papers. You should be, in a humble way, an artist. The programmes are the road and the destination: the BBC is just the vehicle.

But as the twentieth century — the broadcasting century — drew to its close, the wheels of the vehicle started wobbling so violently that it could not be ignored. Under the radically 'modernizing' Director-General John Birt the Corporation became unrecognizable to those who had worked in it for years. Babies — dozens of them — were thrown out with the bathwater. There was a wilful perversity about the direction that the Birt reforms took. Whereas the real faults of the BBC lay in its bureaucracy, and its real glories were its programme-makers, the reforms deftly managed to sideline the creative staff and lard on endless new layers and systems of management, with fatal thrombotic effect.

Sure, they were differently named managers, but they were just as depressing: more so, because they did not even pay lip-service to the old cultural values of the BBC. A worship of 'consultants' and theorists was coupled with the notion of permanent revolution — John Birt once proudly told me, when I asked when the structure would settle down and stop changing shape, that the answer was 'Never!'

His thinking bore such fruit as the illogical and wasteful 'internal market', the rundown of the craft base, and the cheapening or eradication of resources like libraries and archives. The old idea of common resources and a common purpose, of the BBC as almost a university, was junked. News libraries, archives, gram library — everything had to be bought and paid for on ever-tighter budgets. Systems arose whereby it became too expensive for a programme to get out a disc from the gram library, or consult the library properly, because such things were charged for, per item, through a vast wasteful bureaucracy.

Staffing reforms, designed to end smugness, ended security instead, and chipped away at creativity. A new and nervy generation of producers appeared, and a community of gifted, highly qualified but woefully short-contract researchers who were never sure whether it was wise to 'waste' a good idea by mentioning it to a Corporation which regarded them as disposable.

Everything had a price, nothing had a value. Budgets for research and content of programmes were cut, while a few fashionable star names were paid absurdly, and managers' bonuses shot up. Programme-makers — apart from a favoured few in television — were treated with arch contempt by not very talented managers. Budget cuts were universal during those years, to pay for News 24 and the new digital channels to come; but a cut in resources inevitably hits radio harder. In a comparatively simple, cheap medium there is no fat to trim. Every cut immediately affects output. Put Billy Bunter and Kate Moss on the same starvation diet, and Bunter will get thinner but Kate Moss will die.

The general Birtian restructuring and contracting-out also threatened radio skills more than television. If you are shedding a lot of your craft base, your technical core, and losing squads of experienced programme-makers, then in the television world this is not an irretrievable error. Other people may well pick them up. And when you come to your senses again you can hire them — or those they taught — back. There's lots of television being made out there, and you cannot name any type of programme BBC Television makes (except perhaps those for schools) which is not replicated somewhere by a commercial channel. BBC and commercial TV now buy from the same production outfits, and fight for the same US programming. There is no technique that BBC Television has developed which is not also needed and practised by commercial television. On radio, the same goes for disc jockeys (and news jockeys too, up to a point).

But Radio 4's type of programming (in which I include parts of Radios 2, 3 and 5, and the World Service) has no commercial counterpart. If the BBC doesn't run a crafted, quality, cerebral, cultured radio service, then nobody will. Commercial radio will always tend to be music and the very cheapest forms of talk, usually unedited. The BBC knows this. It is why Radio 4 can be such a pain to deal with. You say to a commissioning authority there, 'Look — I have this perfect radio idea!' but you know, and they know, that there is only one possible buyer for that idea, and if they won't take it it is dead — unless you convert it to television, thus losing what made it unique. There are signs now of digital commercial speech radio emerging: I wish it speed, because the best thing in the world for BBC Radio would be if it had a proper, heavy-hitting rival to protect the craft itself. But it will always be fiendishly difficult to fund quality speech radio with advertising.

Other dangerous things happened under John Birt. Departments were stripped of their power, good staff sacked and contract workers shabbily treated, and a crazily inflated hierarchy of 'commissioning editors' was imposed. Beyond that, the cult of 'bi-mediality' meant that news reporters had to work across both radio and TV, with the result that instead of proper radio reports on the six o'clock radio news you would

273

often hear what was effectively just the soundtrack of a TV report. News staffs — especially correspondents — became hopelessly stretched by the proliferation of new channels after 5 Live and News 24 appeared, and complained of having to spend their time hastily scanning official reports and repeating themselves over and over in studios, instead of going out and discovering solid truth.

So Broadcasting House was, for a few years, an uncomfortable place, and I was frankly glad to be only a weekly visitor, nipping in for *Midweek* and the education programme and escaping the next day. One of the most distressing aspects of it was that decent producers, with taste and wit, found themselves seduced into managerial jobs where they had to disguise both qualities in order to survive and keep their mortages paid.

There are few things sadder than sitting opposite someone you know to have discernment and skill and understanding, and to hear him spouting unspeakable jargon from the latest Birtifesto. ('We shouldn't be serving the audience we have — we should be *shocking* them, and reaching out to an audience which has never heard of us.' And this from people who lectured you constantly on the importance of the market economy.) I met an old *Today* friend recently, and asked him what he had been doing in the last few years. 'I joined the bastards,' he said rather sadly. 'I talked utter bollocks for three years, and sacked people. Now I've left and rejoined the human race. But I'm not proud.'

Hosts of others, who should today have been the solid gold core of the BBC, passing on vision and values and craft, took early retirement at fifty.

The old BBC used to grow — in sometimes alarming profusion — a type which Stephen Poliakoff calls 'Oswalds', after the elaborately dysfunctional, anorakish figure played by Timothy Spall in his drama series about a threatened photo library. An Oswald is someone who holds the soul of an institution in his hands; who cares passionately about the detail and the tradition and the wonder of what he deals with, and has to be tolerated by the management even though he's not a corporate man and keeps breaking rules. The BBC had many Oswalds once; donnish, otherworldly figures protected, though not very highly paid, because they did detailed jobs with passion.

There was no place for Oswalds in the new order. Like the Picts, they were driven out or driven underground. A few survive still: but where radio did escape some of the cultural damage of these years, it was for the depressing reason that the top management thought only of television and at times mercifully forgot that speech radio existed. TV executives, in fact, traditionally regard radio as a sort of larval, incomplete version of television, and despise it accordingly.

The sorrow of it all was that when dense, serious, witty, erudite programmes got made, it was largely in spite of the structures and systems of the Corporation itself. In the nineties I watched talented producers sacrifice aeons of their own time to research which in former times they would have got help with; they did it simply because they could not bear to do less than the best.

★ ★ ★

At the height of this misery I was persuaded to make a speech to the Radio Academy proposing the motion 'that the BBC is no longer a fit guardian of quality speech radio'. I took as an image the statue of Prospero sending out Ariel on the front of Broadcasting House. We all know Prospero; we walk under him every time we go into Broadcasting House, just before we get to the inscription about this temple to the Arts and Sciences being dedicated to Almighty God.

Usually the image in one's mind is of the wizard releasing Ariel — 'now to the elements be thou free'. But, I said, there was something about the Prospero in the BBC's theme park exhibition in the basement (now closed) which bothered me. He didn't look benevolent. There he was, big powerful Prospero; and it seemed that he had put his hands on the naked child's shoulders and tightened them. As if he was going to strangle the boy . . .

The gist of what I said was that the unique skills and ethos of UK radio were in grave danger, and so was the very concept of public service radio not based on pop or rolling news. There had been much debate in the preceding months about James Boyle's new schedule, but I thought this a red herring: the really serious thing was that Boyle had felt forced to bring in this new schedule in pursuit of higher ratings; and that the BBC had become so crass that it valued nothing else. It did not — as many continentals do — even bother to do proper qualitative research, with an 'attention index' to see what people actually got from radio. If you work only on raw numbers, inevitably the pop channels will always score higher. They get played in workplaces and factories because they are cheaper than a CD collection. It doesn't mean they're giving anybody much.

I was Cassandra, because it seemed clear to me that the writing was on the wall; the BBC was evolving into a big player in the hawkish global television industry, and could frankly not be trusted with something as thoughtful, unhawkish, adult, discursive, and intellectually adventurous as quality radio. If we were inventing the whole shebang from scratch, I reckoned that radio would have nothing at all to do with the modern TV industry, any more than you would put Kelvin MacKenzie in charge of a Cambridge college or hand over the Royal Shakespeare Company to Disney. I mourned for the old core values of public service: rigour, intellectual curiosity, and a sense of common cultural inheritance. This is vital: sometimes the defenders of Radios 4 and 3 compare them to things like opera, or ballet, or symphony orchestras, which may be élite but which are considered worth preserving for the sake of the culture at large. Yet radio is *more* worth

277

preserving because it is free to all, all the time.

I know people with no money, minimal social status and basic education — the older ones left school at fourteen — who like to listen, as of right, to important contemporary scientists and historians and actors and artists talking about their knowledge and their craft. I know people who have never been to London, who work with their hands, yet can make as sophisticated a joke as any you'll hear in Notting Hill. They're up to speed, they're in the swim. BBC Radio plugs them in to everything worth hearing. These people — and OK, there are not nearly as many of them as there are pop and TV addicts — will say to you that radio is their university, and their friend.

All this, I said, was being gradually thrown away, because if the TV and radio services were once brothers in the BBC family, now Cain had been given the key to Abel's life-support machine. From the floor, a Birt executive, Matthew Bannister, sneered: 'Some people are always afraid of change.' Which was as unfair as you would expect. After all, I was the one who was advocating change, a radical new kind of ownership and management for radio. What I feared was not change but degradation, dumbing to infinity, institutional contempt and chronic starvation of intellectual resources. It seemed to me then that the only hope for radio's future as an intelligent medium in the UK was for it to be removed from the present BBC structure and its bosses, ring-fenced, allocated a modest budget and given its freedom.

That was 1999. I wanted to be proved wrong. I wanted it to be possible for the letters 'BBC' to remain letters on a radio microphone. Those letters have meant a great deal for a long time. They belong to the radio tradition more deeply, in fact, than to television. They belong to the age of Reith, who for all his absurdities knew in his bones that the best use of this marvellous technology, these aerial spears against the sky, is to broadcast into every home 'all that is best in every department of human knowledge, endeavour and achievement'. That is what you breathe in the air of Broadcasting House, which as John Humphrys once remarked is 'a building which makes certain demands on you' (although it was only months after that splendid line that they moved him and the *Today* programme to White City).

But what is this? Spring may have come, and the White Witch's grip of eternal winter is loosened. Things are looking up. Today, as the twenty-first century gets well under way, things look brighter for radio. Its listening figures are soaring as television's decline. Within the BBC itself attitudes have markedly changed; it is not uncommon now for a senior radio job to be contested by TV veterans dismayed by the new demands of their own medium ('It's Celebrity Sleepover with Vanessa Feltz!') and longing to do something different. The arrival of Helen Boaden at Radio 4 and Jenny Abramsky as Managing Director Radio brings back to the forefront the survivors of my own *Today* generation, which whole-heartedly believed in the medium. It seems, happily, that their time under John Birt left them at least the major part of their thinking and feeling apparatus.

Lord Birt himself has moved on. Greg Dyke, a populist and practical figure, replaced him and promptly removed quite a lot of the nonsensical Birtian managerialist structures (though as I write, the job is not finished). The impression, at least, is given that Mr Dyke listens to staff and wants ideas to come up from the ground, rather than down from management theory. There is encouragement in the breezy style of his round-robin e-mails and 'cut the crap and make it happen' campaign. If in some obscure radio office, you push the 'reply' button after one of his general e-mails and take him on, you will eventually get a personal reply. Problems remain, and always will, and the short-contract culture continues to put unnecessary stress on some very talented young people (though Greg Dyke promised reform here too). It is better than it was. A sense of relaxation and fun is gradually returning to the radio departments.

Above all, radio's popular resurgence has made the BBC senior management notice that it has a jewel in its possession. Amid all the debate over the fairness of the licence fee in a multi-channel, soon-to-be-digital TV world, BBC Radio is accepted as excellent value, including its newest channels 5 Live and 6 Music. We still do not have a proper measure of the value of speech radio (again, I point enviously to the continental system of measuring not only whether the radio is on, but whether anyone is paying any attention to it), but at least the ratings are up.

Moreover, I think the argument over raw figures is slowly being won. You can't control speech radio ratings in simplistic television ways. Buying big stars rarely helps, and American imports would not help at all. Nor would the TV mindset in which well-educated and cultured people rush to produce programmes that they themselves would never condescend to watch. To run radio you must be more like an old-fashioned publisher, a 1930s Gollancz or Faber & Faber, working on faith and idealism and wanting to share what you yourself love. All that you can do is to make — and publicize — the best and most passionately well-crafted pro-grammes you can think of. Ratings have to be watched, but calmly and with a sense of proportion. You have to believe that if even one person is swayed, or inspired, or changed, or comforted, by a programme, then that pro-gramme has been worthwhile.

20

And Now . . .

I have presented *Midweek*, as I write, for nearly two decades: longer than all my other radio jobs put together. Another regular job, over the past few years, has been the Tuesday afternoon education programme now known as *The Learning Curve*, in which I am the mouthpiece and figurehead for an exhilaratingly bright team of researchers. Sometimes it is like doing a GCSE myself every week, assimilating reams of material on prison education, or government policy, or literacy research.

The two programmes have, for the past year or so, shared an office, a tiny but desirable space with a roof terrace high above the statue of Prospero on the bow of Broadcasting House. It is a very good place from which to view anti-globalization protesters being herded into Oxford Circus. We shall miss it when they throw us out for yet another planned revamp of Broadcasting House.

The shared office means that sometimes on a Tuesday afternoon I get producers and researchers in stereo, one lot shouting data about Key Stage 2 education targets and the other informing me that some pestilential celebrity has cancelled and will be replaced by a theatrical wig technician. It is a demanding and highly entertaining way of spending Tuesdays, and leaves me fit for nothing much by evening.

But despite this cosy Tuesday base, I remain a freelance. Over the last decade I have made a few more radio documentaries, with particularly happy memories of the intricate *Mysterious Ways* which tried to track the influences of Christianity over the last thousand years. For a while in the early nineties I still presented *Sunday*, but was dropped from it in the uniquely cavalier BBC way (they just omit to re-book your dates one month, and then sound pained and surprised when you ring to check, as you have been doing every month for the past two years). It is worth mentioning in passing that BBC people are culturally odd this way: they have, for instance, always had a habit of doing 'availability checks' and asking people to pencil in dates, then changing their mind and forgetting to call them off. Commercial broadcasters rarely do this. Oddest of all, years ago I did two pilot programmes for a new book quiz, and was told that it went fine and they 'hoped to get a series the next winter'. Nothing happened. I forgot all about it. Then one day, in the car, I heard the announcement of a new series, with the familiar signature tune and titles, but a different presenter. The producer hadn't bothered to tell me that, yes, he had got the commission — but no, not with me.

Go to any gathering of BBC freelances anywhere, and you will hear similar stories. One woman was left hanging on for a year on the understanding that she would present a legal magazine programme on BBC TV: the first she knew of their change of mind was the *Radio Times* billing for her replacement. Long after the demise of Reithian values, Reithian arrogance remains. *We are the BBC: you should be honoured that we even thought of you, even briefly*. Sometimes, people who have spent a lifetime working for the BBC are astonished to find that they can be dropped for good, without a word. Ray Gosling, for years a well-liked and interestingly quirky *auteur* of 100 television documentaries and over 1,000 radio programmes, expressed elegant outrage in 2002 when the drying-up of his work (combined with a certain amount of personal chaos) drove him to bankruptcy. He did, however, get to make a TV documentary about going bankrupt. Years earlier, I helped on a documentary about the life-work of Monty Modlyn, who again was a familiar radio figure for twenty-odd years. We made a tribute to him, *Modlyn Through*, and I fear he may have hoped it was a re-launch. It wasn't. When they've spat you out, you stay spat.

I pass these things on merely to emphasize the precariousness and looseness of the position held by any freelance in the trade. People often ask me if I can give their children jobs (I have less power to do so than Sooty), and they also think that the voices of the BBC are somehow 'part of it', with power and influence over its management. Not so: we are, as Robert Robinson once put it, merely the hired hands. But I have no resentment about any of this: I chose to be free, not part of the Corporation system, and I have done fine. I like my colleagues, I respect quite a few of the management (though not all). I mention the quirks in BBC treatment of freelances merely because they are behaviours widely known within the trade, and rarely publicized because people are nervous of offending Auntie. They are not new or modern behaviours: they lie deep in the culture. At the end of his 1972 book *The Biggest Aspidistra in the World* Peter Black offers a wonderful and still wholly accurate description of the BBC mindset:

> It is capable of a stony cruelty to people it has decided are no longer valuable. They are un-personed . . . few organizations produce as many masters of the art of suddenly letting their glance focus just past an approaching person whom it would be inconvenient to notice. It courts its enemies and despises its friends, on whom it heaps the crudest and most insulting flattery. You can be close to the BBC for twenty years and suddenly find it turning upon you the face of a secret society that you realize you know nothing about.

I should hastily say that Peter Black goes on to praise the Corporation's 'inner artistic integrity' as incorruptible. That was in 1972.

This book has been, in great part, about being a broadcaster. But actually, like anybody else, I am a listener first and foremost and that is why I wanted to write it. The joy of radio was beautifully expressed in early 2002 by Simon Jenkins, *The Times* columnist and former editor. He said that Radio 4, in particular, has never been better than today:

> The modulation of its news magazines is masterful. Radio drama and documentary have reformed forms of art and journalism that are virtually dead in the commercial sector. On a recent weekend I found myself listening, roughly in sequence, to a reading of Byron's love letters, a debate on the Geneva Conventions and a satirical diary 'borrowed' from *Pride and Prejudice*. All assumed an educated and attentive audience and were produced with panache.

He went on to quote Marshall McLuhan, describing radio's potency as that of 'the tribal drum'.

> It was more than a mobile medium of music and chat. 'Cool' television was a calming, dumbing, enervating medium. 'Hot' radio was intimate, active, angry. By compelling the attention of just one sense, that of hearing, it required a mental concentration not required for television. Appear on radio and people remember what you say. Appear on television and they notice your tie . . . (radio) forms the backdrop to the lives of millions, young and old. It is a perpetual nervous stimulus, exciting furious passions.

His point about the expectations of radio, its demands, came piquantly just before a rumpus when Gavyn Davies, the BBC Chairman, got into hot water with a speech accusing 'white, middle-class, educated, middle-aged' people of hijacking the BBC and 'consuming' more than their share of it. The most striking thing to me was the oddity of using the metaphor of consumption in this context. For the wonderful thing about broadcasting is that however many people 'consume' it, the whole product remains free, and fresh, for all. It is never in shortage: therefore we can afford joyfully to make it the very best we can.

For all its faults, good speech radio — on whichever channel — is a marvel: offering direct communication, mind to mind, democratic and portable. Think how usefully and amusingly it fills the interstices of a busy day. For the long-distance driver, the homeworker, the craftsman, or — as I know from experience — the patient in a hospital bed recovering from double eye surgery it is a precious thing to switch on, maybe just for the News, and end up accidentally better-informed about Icelandic sagas or the medieval church or particle physics. Or urine. You would not get any TV station risking half an hour on the history of industrial uses of urine, but it was a great radio programme.

The other day — an ordinary day — spent making a long journey home by train and car and then cooking a meal, opening routine post and packing a bag for another journey, I lived almost all the while in another, parallel world. I caught up with the news, learnt some seventeenth-century history, meditated on the Hindu concept of Jesus, shouted furiously at a bigot or two, was moved to tears by the conclusion of a monologue drama by Lynn Truss about rival sisters, and then startlingly educated by an unpretentious little programme on the history of the stethoscope.

The latter was a particularly good example of what radio does best, because medical information works better on radio (less goo, less obstructive 'yuk' factor), and also because the intensity of the doctor's experience in listening for different heart sounds could be evoked by playing them to an equally 'blind' listenership. It also, with all the unselfconsciousness of a discreet medium, included some enlighteningly giggly reflections by a doctor on the stethoscope as a badge of office — 'my little comfort blanket'.

She might not have been quite as honest with a camera trained on her. Anyway, how on earth would a programme on the history of the stethoscope ever fight its way through the layers of anxiety, ratings-greed and financial stress of a TV commissioning system? And who would really want to sit down and watch it, passive in an armchair? But I learnt from it, and remember it keenly.

Yet all the time that my mind dwelt on stethoscopes, sisterhood, Hindu theology and public affairs I was physically busy, travelling and dealing with the irritating minutiae of daily life.

Music radio might have soothed or invigorated me, and inane disc-jockey chat could have been some sort of ersatz 'company'. But what this neo-Reithian kind of radio did was actually to double the usefulness and value of that day in my life, making me laugh and think and mentally explore. It made the dull physical jobs tolerable, and fitted me better for the mental ones to come. It made me more alive.

What could be more precious? Or more worth fighting for?

Index

Hislop, Ian 260
Hoggart, Simon 234
Holland, Julian 241-2
Hollingsworth, Mike
156-7, 159
Hood, Stuart, quoted 32-3
Horsley, William 41-5
House, Gordon 51, 53
Howe, Geoffrey 215
Humphrys, John 140, 207,
279

Ingham, Bernard 222
Ingrams, Richard 260
Innes, Michael 127-8
HMS Invincible, Today
programme from 225-8

James, Dame Naomi 176-7
James, Rob 176-7
Jenkins, Simon, quoted 286
Junor, Sir John 268

Kelly, Henry 256
Kings' Singers 154-5
Kitchen, Gordon 98

Langham, Portland Place
49, 50
training studios 52-7
Lewis, Captain C. A. 15,
18-9
Lewis-Smith, Victor 194,
260
Linley, David, Lord 263,
265
Livesey, Captain 226,
227-8

Lunn, Sally 177
Lynam, Desmond 138-9,
140

McIntyre, Ian 180-1, 183,
184
MacKenzie, Kelvin 263-4
Macmillan, Laurie 183
McNicholas, Brenda 93-4
Marconi company 13
Martin, Bryan 183
Maxwell, Robert 267
Mellor, David 142, 164
Midweek programme 254-
8, 259-69
Modlyn, Monty 284
Monson, Jolyon 143
Murray, John 153, 162
musicians' unions, 'Needle-
time' agreement 90

Naughtie, James 140, 261
Newbury, John (Revd)
245, 246, 247, 249
non-needletime music (NNT)
90-1
Norbrook, Donald 96-7,
98-100
Norman, Barry 138, 140,
158

O'Rahilly, Ronan 28
Osborne, Alistair 144
'Oswalds' 275

Payne, Dennis 119, 163
Perkins, Brian 183
phone-ins 87

293

Other titles in the
Charnwood Library Series:

EATERS OF THE DEAD

Michael Crichton

In A.D. 922 Ibn Fadlan, the representative of the ruler of Bagdad, City of Peace, crosses the Caspian Sea and journeys up the valley of the Volga on a mission to the King of Saqaliba. Before he arrives, he meets with Buliwyf, a powerful Viking chieftain who is summoned by his besieged relatives to the North. Buliwyf must return to Scandinavia and save his countrymen and family from the monsters of the mist . . .

THE SAVAGE SKY

Emma Drummond

1941: Rob Stallard, the unworldly son of a farmer, leaves war-torn London for a Florida airbase along with a group of RAF pilot cadets. He quickly develops a great passion and talent for flying, but is not so happy when he encounters US cadet James Theodore Benson III, son of a senator. Rob is instantly averse to a man who appears to regard flying as merely another string to his sporting bow. For his part, Jim sees Rob as a 'cowpoke from Hicksville'. Personal dislike rapidly extends to professional rivalry, and a near-fatal flying incident creates bitter enmity between them that will last more than a decade.

THE UGLY SISTER

Winston Graham

The Napoleonic Wars have ended as Emma Spry tells her fascinating story . . . One side of her face marred at birth, Emma grows up without affection, her elegant mother on the stage, her father killed in a duel before she was born. Her beautiful sister, Tamsin, is four years the elder, and her mother's ambitions lie in Tamsin's future, and in her own success. A shadow over their childhood is the ominous butler, Slade. Then there is predatory Bram Fox, with his dazzling smile; Charles Lane, a young engineer; and Canon Robartes, relishing rebellion in the young Emma, her wit, her vulnerability, encouraging her natural gift for song.